The
No-Time-To-Cook Book

By Janet B. Chadwick

A Garden Way Publishing Book

Storey Communications, Inc.
Pownal, VT 05261

Designed by Cindy McFarland

Copyright © 1986 by Janet B. Chadwick

All rights reserved. No part of this book may be produced without written permission from the publisher, except by a reviewer who may quote brief passages or reproduce illustrations in a review with appropriate credits; nor may any part of this book be reproduced, stored in a retrieval system, or transmitted in any form or by any electronic means, mechanical, photocopying, recording, or other, without written permission from the publisher.

The name Garden Way Publishing has been licensed to Storey Communications, Inc. by Garden Way, Inc.

Printed in the United States by Hamilton Press

Second Printing, August, 1986

Library of Congress Cataloging-in-Publication Data

Chadwick, Janet, 1933 —
    The no time to cook book.

    "A Garden Way Publishing book."
    Includes index.
    1. Cookery. I. Title
TX652.C476   1986   641.5'55   85-70194
ISBN 0-88266-393-3

TABLE OF CONTENTS

Saving Time 1
    1 Tools of the Trade 3
    2 Tips for Smart Cooks 27
    3 Chain Cooking 35
    4 Using the Weekly Menu Plan 53

Recipes 59
    1 Homemade Mixes 61
    2 Bread and Rolls 71
    3 Soups 85
    4 Casseroles and Side Dishes 97
    5 Fish 115
    6 Poultry 123
    7 Beef, Pork, and Lamb 135
    8 Salads and Dressings 147
    9 Sauces and Dips 153
    10 Desserts 159

Appendices 175
    Suggested Substitutions 175
    Pantry Staples 177
    Glossary 178
    More Menus 180

Index 183

SAVING TIME

Time — there never seems to be enough of it. We're constantly juggling career, community, family, friends, home, and self, and something always gets short shrift. Despite our best intentions, we sometimes shortchange ourselves and our families when it comes to nutrition and well-prepared meals. We stop at fast-food and take-out restaurants on the way home, or we buy junk food or poorly prepared frozen dinners — anything quick and easy — so that we can get dinner on the table in minutes.

We pay for this in more ways than one. First, fast foods are expensive, and, because they are not packed with good quality protein, fiber, and complex carbohydrates, we get hungry a lot faster and tend to overeat. Second, fast foods are usually packed with saturated fats and sodium, which can lead to high blood pressure, obesity, and cardiovascular disease.

In this book I'm going to show you how to save time in the kitchen, so that you don't have to resort to fast-food restaurants and frozen dinners. I'm going to give you wholesome, good-tasting, and easy-to-prepare recipes that do not take hours. You will be able to take your own prepared-in-advance basic foods and add to them quickly and easily so that a good dinner can be on the table in thirty to forty minutes.

You will find recipes for old favorites that you thought took a long time to prepare, such as fricassee of chicken, pot roast with vegetables, and roast duckling. By doing one step in the morning or the night before, you can prepare these special dinners in half an hour or less when you get home from work — and relax with your family or guests in the time saved.

Even if you prepare only sauces, mixes, and vegetables in advance, you will save hours of work each week. You will also save money, since rarely does anything go to waste.

For years experts have been studying how to increase efficiency in offices, factories, schools, and even social activities. I'm suggesting that time management can be moved into the kitchen with the same effectiveness. With other family members involved, the work can go even faster and be loads of fun. This book will make an expert out of even the most inexperienced cook.

Having the right equipment is just as important in the kitchen as it is in an office or laboratory. You can't be efficient without it. The tools of the trade make life easier and give you extra time to spend with your family and to do other things that you enjoy. In this book, you will learn how to make maximum use of your appliances.

Here are some general hints for getting the most out of this book:

☐ Read the entire book at least once before trying any of the recipes — many of them depend on techniques explained elsewhere in the book.

☐ Much of the time-saving in this book depends on appliances such as the food processor and slow-cooker. (See Chapter 1.) In particular, many of my bread recipes depend on the use of a food processor to mix the dough.

☐ In many instances, I give quantities of ingredients in ounces and pounds instead of cups. The use of a small kitchen scale will give you consistently good results.

☐ For best results, use the size dish recommended in the recipe when it is specified.

☐ Unless I state otherwise, fresh, frozen, or canned vegetables may be used in the recipes.

☐ I often recommend that a quantity of food be tray-frozen. This means placing pieces of food separately on a cookie sheet to freeze, so that they won't freeze in a clump. Once frozen, they can be dumped into a freezer-safe plastic bag for keeping.

☐ Greasing your casserole dishes and baking pans is faster with a vegetable oil spray — I rely on them. They make clean-up faster and easier, too.

This book is for people who rank the health and happiness of their families at the *same* level as their careers or personal pleasures. It's both for people who love to cook and for those who would never set foot in a kitchen if they didn't have to. And it's definitely for those who enjoy challenges and aren't afraid to try something new.

CHAPTER 1
TOOLS OF THE TRADE

If you are serious about preparing tasty meals quickly and easily, you should consider investing in some time-saving equipment. You may have most of these products already. If you haven't, you can buy a good sturdy blender, a food processor, and two (yes, I said two) slow-cookers, all for around $100. This equipment will pay for itself in savings from your food budget in just a matter of months, especially if you have a large family.

It isn't necessary to purchase the most expensive equipment on the market; there are reliable products at reasonable prices. A good food processor, for example, is the best helping hand a busy person can have. You can pay $300 or more for the best models of the Cuisinart or Robo-Coupe or about $40 for the General Electric FP-1. On the other hand, every new gadget that comes along is not worth the money. Make sure that any new appliance is going to do something for you that *needs to be done* and can't be done by an appliance you already own.

Before buying any equipment, you should consider what kinds of meals your family prefers. If they like roasts, casseroles, stews, and soups, you will need a slow-cooker, roasting pans (large and small), large stock pots, and oven-safe baking dishes of various sizes (preferably freezer-to-oven-safe). If they prefer stir-fry meals or other top-of-the-stove cooking, such as deep frying, a good investment would be heavy cast-iron or Silverstone-coated aluminum skillets of various sizes, and possibly a large steel wok. (Cast-iron skillets get my vote every time, and they are less expensive than club aluminum.)

Appliances

In my kitchen, I have found that the most time-saving large appliances are my freezer, microwave oven, and dishwasher. You can prepare good meals without them, but these appliances will save you both time and money. They will probably pay for themselves many times over because you are able to make such good use of every penny's worth of food you purchase. You can buy in quantity, cook in quantity, and cook ahead for quick and easy meals, for special dietary problems and for company meals that need only to be taken from the freezer and put into the oven, leaving you free to enjoy your guests.

Freezers

Freezers are a major investment, and you should shop for them wisely. A good freezer can be purchased from a large chain store such as Sears, Montgomery Ward, or Penney's for as much as one-third less than some of the brand-name products — but even at these stores you need to shop for the most energy-efficient models.

Small freezers inside refrigerators are not cold enough to freeze and store food for long periods; these units were meant for storage for two to three weeks at best. The most efficient way to use such a freezer is to move the food that you will need for a few days or a week at a time from your large freezer to the refrigerator freezer. This will make your large freezer more efficient because you will not be opening it as often. For long-term storage, your freezer must maintain a temperature of 0° F. or below.

BASIC KITCHEN EQUIPMENT

A variety of paring knives, large-blade chopping knives, and serrated bread knives
A cutting board
Strainers: a fine sieve and large colanders
Heavy, covered saucepans, small to large sizes
A large soup kettle or stock pot
Heavy cast-iron or similar weight frying pans of several sizes
Mixing bowls of many sizes

Storage containers for refrigerator and freezer: food-safe plastic bags and boxes, freezer wrap or foil, and freezer-safe jars and casserole dishes
Pyrex measuring cups of several sizes
Plastic or metal cups for measuring dry ingredients
Cookie sheets and muffin tins
Cake and pie plates, preferably Pyrex (these require lower baking temperatures)

Bread and meat-loaf pans
A kitchen scale
Measuring and mixing spoons
A large slotted spoon
Wire cooling racks
Meat-roasting racks
Wire whisks (indispensable)
Spatulas: rubber for scraping and metal for lifting
A soup ladle
A rolling pin
Meat, candy, and deep-fry thermometers

The cost of running a freezer should be taken into consideration. The new freezers display an energy label to help you calculate the efficiency of each model and compare it with others. Most of the new energy-efficient models cost about $50 a year to operate, and older models may cost $20 to $30 more per year. The life of a freezer is usually estimated at between ten and fifteen years; however, I have one that is twenty-five years old and another that is eighteen years old, and while they have become somewhat rusty on the outside, they still function as well as ever and have never required repair.

Most freezers built today are self-defrosting. They are not necessarily more costly to run than manual-defrost units, because frost accumulates around the cooling coils of the latter type and makes them use more energy.

Most models have a bottom drain to remove the defrost water. Other desirable features to look for are baskets for bulk items (more important for chest freezers), fast-freeze shelves for initial freezing, a light that indicates that the freezer is working properly, and an alarm that sounds if the freezer temperature rises.

Space is often the factor that determines whether you buy a chest freezer or an upright. Small apartments can usually accommodate an upright freezer in some corner. Upright freezers use less floor space and they make reaching for food more convenient, but cold air spills out of them when the door is opened, so their operating costs are higher. Some of the space in an upright freezer is wasted since it must be packed so that food doesn't fall out when the door is opened.

Chest freezers take up a little more floor space, but if you have the room, they are more economical to buy and operate. Chest freezers remain colder than uprights. Because cold air doesn't rise, it doesn't escape when the lid is raised. They hold more food overall per cubic foot, and if you keep good records of what you have in the freezer and in what section it is stored, it won't be any harder to find.

Microwave Ovens

Even if you do not usually like microwave-cooked food (and I do not), once you learn to make the best use of your microwave oven, you will wonder how you ever got along without it. You can reheat food in minutes with the same fresh taste as the originally prepared dish; you can defrost even large pieces of meat (that you forgot to take out for dinner) in a half-hour or less; you can partially bake roasts, casseroles, baked potatoes, and even pies, breads, and rolls, then finish them in a conventional oven in record time.

worlds. For instance, four medium-size potatoes can be prebaked in a microwave oven for about ten minutes while you are preheating your conventional oven to 425° F. Then the potatoes can be popped into the conventional oven for about twenty minutes. This is a total of 30 minutes, half the time for potatoes baked completely in a conventional oven, and the result is the same.

If your family's schedule makes it difficult for everyone to eat at the same time, you will find the microwave oven a big help. Casseroles, soups, stews, and meat-potato-vegetable dinners can be prepared by any method of cooking, any hour of the day or night, and reheated in individual portions for the person who must eat at a different time from the rest of the family. Foods for family members on special diets can also be prepared ahead of time, frozen in individual-serving portions, and quickly defrosted and reheated at meal time, saving the confusion of trying to prepare two different meals at the same time.

Microwave ovens do a wonderful job of sautéing and of making sauces that do not have to be stirred constantly. A microwave defrosts and reheats dinner rolls in seconds. Once you start using one, you will find many other uses for it as well. The combination of freezer and microwave oven gives you a fast-food restaurant in your own home, for far less money and with a much better quality of food.

There are many good brands of microwave ovens on the market. Check out the chain stores. It is not necessary to have a model with many options to perform the tasks I suggest in this book. The oven should be large enough to accommodate casserole dishes and roasts for your family. It should have at least two levels of power (low and high), and it would be nice if it had a defrost cycle, even though you can defrost on low power. Timers and memory banks are extras that are convenient but not necessary, and they cost a great deal more. Look for the newer models with rotating disks or other features to ensure even cooking, so that you don't have to rotate the dish every few minutes yourself. (Rotating disks can be purchased for older models for as low as $35.) Do not purchase a combination microwave-convection oven; it will do neither job well.

Dishwashers

Even though we are down to a family of two, I find my dishwasher indispensable in my busy life. When I prepare foods, I usually prepare enough of the main-course items, as well as extras, for my entire week's menus. This takes many dishes and utensils. I don't like to clean up any more than anyone else does, and using my dishwasher keeps clean-up time to a minimum. During the week, my husband and I simply rinse off our dishes after meals and load them in the dishwasher; when it's full enough (sometimes not for two or three days), we turn it on (making it economical as well).

A study done a few years ago indicated that people who use dishwashers use less hot water than those who rinse their dishes under hot running water as they are washed. Recently I added up the time it took me to do dishes by hand for the two of us for three meals. By the time I took out equipment, filled the sink, washed, rinsed, and stacked the dishes to dry, I had used up one hour and eight minutes for just one day. Because I didn't want to take time to dry the dishes, I left them drying on a shelf, covered with a towel. This took up my shelf space for most of the day, and my kitchen never looked completely clean. I could find many better ways to use an hour or more each day.

Dishwashers can also be used to warm plates and to keep them warm until serving time for a dinner party. And because dishwashers are insulated, they will keep large amounts of food cold or hot for a party (see p. 18). My dishwasher is as close to a maid as I will ever get.

Good dishwashers are put out by many manufacturers. To be most useful, a dishwasher should have a pots-and-pans cycle, a choice of hot or cool dry cycles, and a revolving top spray arm for the top rack. A special plate-warming cycle and a prewash cycle are convenient but not necessary; other cycles can be used for the same purposes. The top rack should not revolve; such racks hold fewer dishes and tend to break glassware as they turn. Again, the large chain stores sell good quality dishwashers at lower prices than the brand-name models.

Small Appliances

Do not purchase a small appliance that functions as several appliances in one, such as a food center that has a blender, slicer, mixer, food chopper, and dough hooks, but only a two-speed motor, or a slow-cooker that also serves as a grill and a deep-fat fryer. These appliances seldom do a good job of *any* of the tasks for which they were designed.

Food Processors

Leading the list of small appliances important to the busy person's kitchen is, without question, the food processor. Food processors work so fast that in just a few minutes you can dice enough onions, green peppers, celery, and carrots for all of your cooking for a month. This versatile appliance combines many of the functions of the blender, grinder, and slicer, and is the single exception to the warning in the preceding paragraph. While processors do not purée as efficiently as blenders, if you can't afford both, they do a pretty creditable job. They will also grind coffee and meat, and slice, shred, grate, and chop vegetables, fruits, hard cheese, and nuts. Many have accessories, available as extras, that will slice thick and shred coarsely, slice very thin and shred fine, cut ripples, cut julienne, and cut French fries. They will also make bread and rolls, pie crust, pizza crust, and sandwich fillings. If you like to preserve extras in the summertime, they make short work of even the hardest tasks. Relishes are so easy you won't believe it!

With all these features, they do have some drawbacks. For instance, who wants to take 5 minutes to clean a processor just for chopping a half-cup of onions? Well, no one does, and that's where proper use comes in. Instead of chopping a half-cup of onions, you chop four cups of onions and several other vegetables at the same time. It might take fifteen minutes of scrubbing and peeling to prepare the vegetables, but with ten minutes' chopping time (at most) and five minutes' clean-up time (most processor parts are dishwasher safe), you can pop the extra vegetables into the freezer and won't have to chop again for a week or two. That's time management and the proper use of your appliances.

What about the extra moisture in vegetables that are chopped in quantity, frozen, and then sautéed? Some will say, "My recipes all come out soggy." To avoid this, simply reduce the amount of moisture or fat called for in the recipe. Fat is sometimes used to flavor a recipe, but often more fat is called for than is needed for flavor in order to keep vegetables from browning or sticking. Reduce the fat, using only about one teaspoon per serving, and cook the vegetables until all excess moisture is evaporated.

There are two types of food processors: the direct-drive processor, in which the work bowl and processing blades sit directly on top of the motor shaft; and the belt-driven processor, in which the work bowl and blades are mounted at one side of the motor.

The direct-drive model will handle heavier doughs easily. It also chops more efficiently and stands up well under frequent use.

The belt-driven processor takes up more space than the direct-drive model. The belt-driven models that I tested overheated quickly, burned out belts often — especially when used to perform several tasks in succession — and could not handle heavy batters such as bread without overheating. I do not recommend this type of processor.

Most food processors feed the diced or sliced vegetables directly into the processor bowl. The larger the bowl, the fewer times you will have to stop to empty it. Some processors have continuous flow chutes that send the processed food directly into a large container on the side. This allows you to process large quantities without stopping to empty the bowl and reassemble the unit. This is especially helpful during the food preservation season; however, it may not be important to you if you do not preserve fruits and vegetables.

While I do not wish to underrate any manufacturer, I do find differences in how well various processors perform, and I feel that my findings could be of value to you. The most expensive processors in each line have oversized feed chutes that accommodate whole fruits and vegetables, such as tomatoes. This is helpful for party cooking, but not important for everyday cooking.

These processors do an excellent job of slicing and shredding; none does a good job of producing a smooth purée. They do not chop well, either, and I suspect this is because the chopping blades are so large and the motors so powerful that the vegetable is overchopped before the blade can come to a stop, even when the pulse button is used properly. This problem may explain why some people say that processor-chopped vegetables are too mushy.

Mid-priced processors that sell for $60 to $90 are more than adequate to the tasks they must perform. The General Electric FP-6 and the Sunbeam La Chef are of especially good quality for the price. They are both direct-drive processors and have the added advantage of a continuous flow chute available as an option.

Accessories for both of these processors include a thin-slice/fine-shred blade, a thick-slice blade, and a french-fry blade. Accessories for all food processors usually include a medium-thick slicing and shredding blade, a steel chopping blade, and sometimes a plastic mixing blade (which I never use).

The quality of the foods processed in the General Electric and the Sunbeam La Chef was average or above. While they did not purée as smoothly as a blender, they both did a good job of puréeing and chopping vegetables. I rate these processors the best buy for the money.

At the bottom of the list in cost, though not in performance, is the General Electric FP-1. It's a noisy little machine, but it does just as good a job as many of the mid-priced processors.

Slow-Cookers (Take two, they're small!)

I'm serious about buying two. The slow-cooker is one of the most time-saving appliances a busy person can own, and models with removable crockery liners can be purchased for under $25. Models without removable crockery liners can often be purchased on sale for as low as $10. One of each would allow you to have complete meat-and-potato dinners ready to serve when you get home at night. The most versatile is the 5-quart size because you can use it to prepare a greater variety of foods, from large batches of soups and sauces to smaller roasts and chickens, whole casseroles, and several baked potatoes.

If you don't like the food you've cooked in a slow-cooker, it's possible that you aren't making the best use of it. I will teach you how to cook in ways that even the manufacturers don't know about. You can cook soups, stews, casseroles (even lasagna), roasts that are moist and juicy, and even baked potatoes. A beef stew started in the morning will be ready to eat when dinner time rolls around. Meats and poultry roasted in a slow-cooker are more flavorful and juicy than those roasted in the oven. There is also less shrinkage because less moisture is lost. I prefer a slow-cooker that sits down into the well of its heating element (the heating coils wind around the outside of the pot). This works much better than a cooker whose pot sits on top of a heating plate. I also prefer a slow-cooker with a removable crockery liner. This type can be used as a casserole dish in a conventional oven or as a serving or storing dish, and it keeps food warm much longer than the thin-wall varieties. A slow-cooker with a removable crockery liner can go into a conventional oven just before serving time to brown roasts or add a crisp topping to a casserole.

Soups, stews, and casseroles can be prepared the night before, stored in the refrigerator in the removable liner, and popped into the slow-cooker before you leave for work in the morning. Dinner will be ready when you get home.

You can operate a slow-cooker for eight hours for approximately the same amount of money that it would cost you to use a 75 watt bulb for one hour. When you come home at night and want to finish browning a casserole or crisping baked potatoes in the conventional oven, you simply place the food in a cold oven and set the temperature for about 400° F. Usually your casserole or potatoes will be finished even before the oven has completely preheated, and you have used very little expensive energy.

Excess moisture, undercooked vegetables, and overseasoned food are the disadvantages most commonly associated with slow-cookers. These problems are easily avoided. The slow-cooker section of this chapter (pp. 19–22) will help you to understand your slow-cooker better and enable you to put it to more efficient use.

My favorite slow-cooker is the Rival Crockpot with a removable crockery liner. I have a 3½- and a 5½-quart cooker, and I use them all the time.

Blenders

Blenders have become a standard appliance in most kitchens. I cannot live without mine and jokingly tell my friends that when my blender breaks down, I go into mourning. Blenders are inexpensive, easy to clean, dishwasher safe, and they can be used to mince, chop, grate, purée, and blend. They are the greatest for smooth purées, sauces, and dressings; and while they are not as efficient as food processors for chopping and shredding food (they chop and shred too fine, and you can do only small amounts at a time), they are okay for a small amount of chopped vegetables if you are caught short.

Prices average between $15 and $30. A multispeed motor (with buttons that indicate the best speed for each process) is better than a single off/on motor. Many blenders come with extra blend/store jars. Most brand-name models, with the exception of the Oster Osterizer, do an excellent job.

The Osterizer blender has a square jar, and the circumference of the blade is not equal to the circumference of the base of this jar, so it is impossible to dry-chop even small amounts of vegetables. There is no way for the vegetables to feed down into the blades. Directions that come with this blender suggest that water be added to the vegetables and then drained off after they are chopped. This leaves you with mushy vegetables that have lost many of their nutrients in the water. The only way to save these nutrients is to use the water in the recipe being prepared, and seldom does a recipe call for this much liquid, unless it is soup.

This blender creates a good vortex with thin liquids; however, the minute a mixture becomes the slightest bit thick, it loses that vortex. It is too lightweight and walks when blending heavier mixtures or when more than half full.

Electric Mixers

Every kitchen should have an electric mixer. It doesn't have to be a large mixer with a base and large bowls that take up shelf space. However, a couple of features should be considered. It should have a motor strong enough to handle heavy batters or mashed potatoes, and beaters should be approximately 2 inches in diameter and made of sturdy stainless steel. Small beaters can take forever to whip or mash. A sturdy, hand-held electric mixer can be purchased for as little as $20. Most small mixers can be mounted on the wall.

Automatic Bag Sealers

Automatic bag sealers and boilable freezer bags can save many hours in the kitchen. Foods prepared in large quantities, such as soups, stews, casseroles, pot roasts with gravy, and fricassee of chicken, can be put in boilable freezer bags in individual portions, sealed with the automatic bag sealer, cooled, and frozen. When needed, these individual portions go quickly from freezer to microwave oven or a pot of boiling water for an effortless meal. You cook only the number of servings needed. There isn't even any clean-up.

If your only experience with foods in boilable bags has been the commercially prepared variety and you have not been pleased with the quality, give this method of food preparation a try in your own kitchen with your own favorite recipes. Often it is the product and the way it was prepared by the manufacturer that are at fault — not the method of food storage.

If you don't want to invest in the sealing unit before trying this system, try sealing the bags with an electric iron set on high and a damp pressing cloth. The sealer works best, but this will give you an opportunity to try this method without spending much money. Look on the package of bags to make certain the bags are boilable. Boilable bags are made of heavy food-safe plastic. Some come in rolls that allow you to cut the size bag you want.

The bags are sealed by placing the top edge of the filled bag on a small sealing strip in the automatic bag sealer. The top bar is lowered and held in place for a few seconds; then the bag can be dropped into cold water to cool quickly. When all the bags are filled, wipe them off and put them in the freezer in a single layer to freeze quickly. You can freeze an entire meal in one bag by placing a portion of meat in the bag, sealing it off, adding a vegetable, sealing it off, adding another vegetable or pasta, and finishing the sealing.

Some manufacturers offer a vacuum-seal feature on their automatic bag sealers; however, since all foods release oxygen after they are sealed, anyway, and you can efficiently remove as much excess air as possible by simply snapping the sides of the bag outward before sealing, this extra feature is a waste of money. My favorite sealer is the Oster automatic bag sealer with touch control. It sells for about $25. It allows you to hold the bag with both hands — just a touch of your little finger lowers the sealing bar. Automatic bag sealers are available from a low of about $10 for the Daizey Seal-a-Meal (always on sale somewhere) to a high of $70 or more for the various models of vacuum sealers. Many automatic bag sealers can be wall mounted.

Automatic Timers

Don't be without one! Never try chain cooking without a timer — the experience will shatter you for life. You do not need an electric timer, but you should have either two or three small timers or one of the multi-project timers that are battery operated and have digital readouts. I prefer the latter. Timed outlets or small units that will turn one of your kitchen outlets into a timed outlet (about $6) are useful if you are away for a very long day. A timed outlet allows you to set the time for an appliance to start or stop cooking.

Nice but Not Necessary

☐ The Daisey Stripper is the nicest little item to come on the market in a long time for large families, people who love to entertain, people who prepare foods in quantity, and people who have any kind of handicap in their hands, such as arthritis. I love it for meal preparation when the whole family is at home. I no longer dread peeling potatoes for 15-20 people when we're all together for the holidays (this almost took the fun out of it for me). It's a very simple, small, electric unit that has a tiny turntable made with four prongs to hold any firm fruit or vegetable. An arm holding a sharp blade is raised and placed against the vegetable, and when the machine is turned on, this blade follows the conformation of any size or shape vegetable or fruit up to 4 inches in diameter. It peels very thinly, leaving most of nutrients intact, and when it gets to the bottom of the vegetable it automatically shuts off.

It doesn't take every blemish off the vegetable — however, while a second potato is peeling (it is not necessary to hold the vegetable), I remove any remaining blemishes from the first one peeled. In this way, I can do 5 pounds of potatoes in a matter of minutes. This item can be purchased for about $25 in most department or hardware stores. If you can't find it, ask if they will order it for you.

☐ An electric ice crusher is handy if you like molded salads or desserts. Molded salads made with crushed ice and a blender take minutes to put together and are ready to eat almost instantly. Using crushed ice instead of ice cubes lessens the risk of damage to your blender blades.

☐ A good electric fry-pan is another handy item to have in the kitchen, especially on chain-cooking days. Large batches of vegetables can be sautéed for casseroles and soups; pot roasts can be braised and sauces simmered, leaving the stove burners free for large soup kettles and other projects. These units also are temperature controlled and will maintain even heat from the high temperatures of deep-fat frying all the way down to the lowest temperatures for braising. This is important when you haven't got time to watch the pot. When shopping for an electric fry-pan, look for one that has a dome cover to accommodate large roasts. It should be submersible for easy cleaning. Prices range from about $25 up.

☐ Electric deep-fry units put out by several manufacturers are handy for families that enjoy deep-fried foods such as fish, chicken, french fries, doughnuts, and egg rolls. The oil can be left in the unit for storage at room temperature. They heat quickly, are temperature controlled, and can be purchased in several sizes, depending on the size of your family. Don't buy the smallest size even if you are a small family or a single person — they are not practical. The very inexpensive models put out by little-known manufacturers do not seem to get hot enough or recover their frying temperatures quickly enough to fry a satisfactory product. I suggest that you stick with a well-known and advertised brand when purchasing this product. The mid-sized units sell for $24–$30.

☐ The Oster 8-quart Super-Pot combines all the features of the above two units, and offers several other features as well. You would not be able to store frying oil in it if you were to use it for other styles of cooking, but that is a minor inconvenience. It's great for quantity-cooking of spaghetti sauces, soups, stews, and boiled dinners and for cooking large batches of spaghetti or corn for a crowd; but it might be too large for the average family. If you are going to cook in quantity, it's a good investment because it's temperature controlled — you don't have to watch the pot. It comes with a baking rack, divided steamer pans, and a deep-fry insert.

☐ A steamer is a handy item to have on hand — I steam-cook most of my vegetables. The quality is better and there is less nutrient loss. They are also handy for reheating cooked rice and pasta and for steaming rolls.

☐ Of the three meat slicers that I tested, I found the Oster to be the best. Made of high-impact plastic (except for the slicing blade), it slices everything from homemade bread to meat and hard cheese. It will not slice frozen foods, however. Its slicing blade adjusts from very-thin-slice to thick-slice, and it comes apart quickly and easily for cleaning. Unfortunately, the parts are not dishwasher safe.

☐ An electric knife makes slicing roasts and fowl quick and easy. This is especially important when preparing large roasts or turkeys to be used for a variety of meals. No one wants to cook all day and then have to struggle with cutting meat into serving-size portions. I was married for thirty-two years before owning one of these helpful tools — now I don't know how I got along without it. You can buy a good electric knife for $15–$20.

☐ The last item I am going to suggest for the busy person's kitchen has nothing to do with food preparation — it is totally for the comfort of the cook. Even in cold weather, I find that when I get going on quantity food preparation, my kitchen gets unbearably warm. When the cook gets overheated, tempers flare, things get broken, the cook often gets burned or cut, and somehow nothing turns out right. A small fan creates just a light breeze to help keep me cool while I overheat the kitchen.

Freezing

Save plastic margarine, yogurt, and cottage cheese **containers** to use as freezer or refrigerator containers. They can be reused many times before breaking down.

☐ ☐ ☐

Purchase a package of 7x9-inch **foil trays** for tray-freezing vegetables in quantity. Foil trays are less expensive than extra cookie sheets that you will not be using for anything else.

☐ ☐ ☐

Make **ice packs** with boilable freezer bags by filling bags with water and freezing them flat on cookie sheets. Use them to keep extra foods cold in portable coolers.

☐ ☐ ☐

Whenever you have several servings of food left over from a meal, seal them in **boilable freezer bags** and freeze, to be reheated in boiling water or a microwave oven for another meal. The flavor and texture will remain good.

☐ ☐ ☐

Leftover tomato paste can be spooned onto an oiled cookie sheet and then frozen in one-tablespoon amounts; **ricotta** and **cottage cheese** can be frozen the same way in half-cup amounts; **soup stocks** and **gravies** can be frozen in ice cube trays in small amounts. Once these foods are frozen, pack them in food-safe freezer bags to be used as needed. Be sure to defrost all these products in a small bowl to retain the juices. (Ricotta and cottage cheese can be used in any recipe in which they will be blended with other ingredients; however, once frozen, they don't stand up well on their own.)

☐ ☐ ☐

Freeze **beef and chicken broth** in ice cube trays to make instant consommé (see page

88), or to use for low-calorie vegetable sautés with a minimum of fat.

□ □ □

Sliced or chopped cooked **meats** should be frozen in broth or gravy to prevent freezer burn.

□ □ □

Freeze **soups** in serving-size containers. This allows you to heat only the amount you need. If you are short of containers, you can pop the soups out of the freezer containers once they are frozen and put them in a large plastic bag.

□ □ □

Soups frozen in boilable freezer bags can go from freezer to office microwave. They will be defrosted by lunchtime and can be reheated right in the pouch, then poured into a cup.

□ □ □

Sandwiches can be made ahead of time and frozen in boilable freezer bags or ziptop bags. They will thaw by lunch. Sandwiches that freeze best are those made with cheese, chicken, meat, peanut butter or nut paste, hard-cooked eggs, or fish. Both slices of bread should be buttered to keep the fillings from making the bread soggy. Do not add mayonnaise or ketchup until just before serving. Lettuce should be wrapped separately in damp paper towels to keep it crisp. Add it just before eating your sandwich.

□ □ □

Sauces made with flour and milk or mayonnaise are not recommended for freezing. Sauces and soups thickened with puréed potato or other vegetables are better. Vegetable sauces will look curdled when defrosted, but they will emulsify beautifully when reheated. Use ½ cup cooked potatoes or other vegetables for each cup of liquid to be thickened.

□ □ □

Line casserole dishes with foil before freezing meals in them. Once the food is frozen (baked or unbaked), lift it out of the casserole dish, overwrap it with foil or freezer paper, and return it to the freezer, freeing your dish for another use.

□ □ □

Special diets can be made more interesting by preparing several different recipes and freezing them in individual portions in boilable freezer bags. The dieter can then have a variety of meals to choose from. These diet meals can be quickly defrosted and reheated in a microwave oven or a pan of boiling water.

Pancakes, waffles, crêpes, and fritters can be made in quantity and tray-frozen. Package in boxes or food-safe plastic bags. Pancakes, waffles, and crêpes can be reheated in a toaster or microwave oven. Fritters can be reheated in a microwave or conventional oven.

□ □ □

Unbaked yeast rolls and breads can be made ahead of time, tray-frozen, sealed individually, and frozen in boilable freezer or zip-top bags. To bake, remove from the bag, allow to rise until double, and bake as usual. Unbaked yeast products are best used within a week.

□ □ □

Homemade cookie doughs can be made up ahead of time and frozen in boilable or zip-top freezer bags. To bake, simply defrost, cut a corner out of the lower part of the bag, squeeze the dough out onto a cookie sheet, and bake as usual. You won't even have a bowl to wash.

□ □ □

To freeze whole **onions** for stews: First, put 2 inches of water in a large roasting pan; cut the tops and bottoms out of four tunafish cans (or cans of similar size); place these in the roaster and put a wire cooling rack on top. Peel whole small onions. Layer the onions two layers deep on the wire rack. Cover the pan, bring the water to a boil, and steam the onions for 6 minutes. Scoop the onions into a bowl of ice water to cool quickly. Drain the onions well. Tray-freeze and then package loosely in food-safe plastic bags. Combinations of vegetables such as carrots, celery, onions, and turnips may be done the same way. These vegetables can be added to a stew during the last 15 minutes of cooking time.

Appliances

In a **looseleaf binder** keep the directions, parts lists, and repair services lists for all your appliances. This will save time when an appliance needs repair.

□ □ □

Read *all* **directions** that come with your appliances even if you have used a similar appliance before. Each manufacturer knows best what a particular appliance will or won't do, and how best to use it.

□ □ □

On any day that you will be cooking several dishes to be refrigerated, **turn the refrigerator to a cooler temperature.** When several warm foods are added in a short period of time, refrigerator temperatures can rise to unsafe levels for the other stored foods. Later in the day, return the temperature to normal.

□ □ □

Foods should *not* be cooled to room temperature before refrigerating. Bacteria starts developing as soon as hot foods cool to below 140 degrees or cold foods warm to above 40 degrees. Therefore, **prompt refrigeration** is not a time-saving factor but a health factor.

□ □ □

House power differs in different parts of the country — it even changes from hour to hour, especially at peak hours of use, when it is usually at its lowest. Electric stoves will take longer to heat and oven temperatures will be harder to maintain at these times. Even microwave intensity is affected by these fluctuations.

□ □ □

On very hot or very cold days, when more electricity is being used, your oven will cook more slowly. You can compensate for this somewhat by **not using any other major appliances** when you are preparing meals.

□ □ □

Test your oven temperature with an **oven thermometer** for accuracy. Not all ovens are set exactly the same. If your oven is set at a temperature other than what the thermometer indicates, adjust all your recipes accordingly.

□ □ □

Clothes dryers are insulated and can be used to keep large amounts of fresh vegetables or beverages cold for a party. Line the dryer with a thick towel to absorb condensation; then top the towel with bags of ice and place vegetables, fruits, or beverages on top of the ice. They will stay cold for several hours.

□ □ □

A **dishwasher** can also be used to keep party foods hot. Place a large cookie sheet across the bottom rack; then add covered dishes of hot foods to the tray. Close the door and set the dishwasher for the last 2 minutes of the hot-dry cycle or plate-warming cycle. Foods will stay hot for an hour or more.

□ □ □

Foods can be kept **cold in the dishwasher** by using a similar method. Place cookie sheets on the bottom rack; then add the food or beverage. Place towels on the top rack and top with bags of ice (see boilable freezer ice bags page 12). The cold will fall (just as heat rises) and keep food and beverages chilled for several hours.

□ □ □

If you heat with a wood stove, keep an **8-quart kettle of water on your stove** for use in your dishwasher. Pour the very hot water into the dishwasher and skip the pots-and-pans cycle as well as the filling part of the normal wash cycle. The water is so hot that it will do a perfect job of cleaning the dishes and will save energy costs as well.

Slow-Cookers

Use canning-jar rings to make a **rack for a slow-cooker** if you do not have one. Place a piece of foil over the screw bands and punch holes in the foil.

□ □ □

In anticipation of an especially long day, your meal can be prepared the night before and **refrigerated overnight in the slow-cooker** (or removable liner if you have one). The cold food plus the cold cooker will take extra time to heat, and this will buy you as much as 2–3 hours extra time.

□ □ □

Use your slow-cooker to serve hot foods or even hot drinks at parties. Try a chocolate fondue in your slow-cooker for a scrumptious party dessert.

□ □ □

If you're making **mashed potatoes for a large crowd,** cook them a little early, mash them, and keep them warm on low in a slow-cooker that has several layers of paper towel placed across the top under the cover. The paper towels prevent condensation from dripping down onto the potatoes. Potatoes will keep warm for 1½–2 hours this way.

□ □ □

To cook dried beans that need presoaking in a slow-cooker, **parboil the beans for 1 full hour** before soaking them, covered, at room temperature, overnight.

□ □ □

Thaw frozen vegetables before adding them to slow-cookers, especially crockery-lined cookers. Frozen foods added to a heated cooker could crack the cooker or ruin the crockery glaze.

□ □ □

Do not lift the cover of your slow-cooker during cooking. When the cover is raised, steam escapes and the cooker may take as long as an hour to recover the proper temperature.

□ □ □

If you are away from home longer than you expected, most slow-cookers connected to a timer will keep food warm at safe levels for about **2 hours after they shut off.**

□ □ □

You can **reheat** food in a slow-cooker with excellent results — even several foods at one time. Much depends on the size of your family and how much you need to reheat. Place the cooked food in **pint jars or coffee cans that have lids.** Put screw lids on tight and then unscrew one turn; punch a small hole in plastic coffee can lids. Put the jars or cans in the slow-cooker and fill the cooker with water up to 2 inches from the tops of the containers. Start with cold water if you will be away all day, or hot tap water if you want the food reheated in 4–6 hours. This is an excellent way to prepare leftovers for your family when you can't make it home in time for dinner.

□ □ □

Use your slow-cooker to make **homemade broths** for rich soups, stews, and sauces. Keep a couple of large food-safe plastic bags in the freezer for bones (one for chicken, one for beef). When you have enough of one kind to fill your slow-cooker, make up a pot of stock (see pp. 85–86). A few minutes to start it one evening and a few minutes to strain it 24 hours later is all the time it takes.

□ □ □

Make up double or triple batches of *Fricassee of Chicken, Beef Stroganoff, Beef Stew, Spaghetti Sauce,* etc. in slow-cookers. Freeze in meal-size portions.

□ □ □

You can **roast small chickens** in a slow-cooker without drying out the drumsticks.

□ □ □

Less tender cuts of meat adapt well to slow-cooker cooking. The meat will be tender, moist, and flavorful, not dry and stringy.

□ □ □

Excessive fat in a recipe or on meat cooked by the slow-cooker method will cause the temperature within the cooker to rise above what it is set for, and foods will cook much faster. **Reduce all fat** in slow-cooker recipes by half. Trim meat of all visible fat.

□ □ □

When slow-cooker recipes call for milk or cream, it's best to add it **during the last half hour** of cooking, so it won't curdle.

□ □ □

For a better appearance, **brown oven-style roasts** in a heavy skillet before cooking in a slow-cooker.

□ □ □

If you have a cooker that has an oven-safe removable liner and you want a crisp topping on your casserole, **remove the liner** from the slow-cooker 20–30 minutes before the casserole is finished, add the topping, and finish the casserole in a conventional oven.

◻ ◻ ◻

The simplest and best sauces for slow-cooker recipes are **canned soups.** Substitute them cup for cup for any sauce called for (see Suggested Substitutions, p. 175). **Omit any salt** called for in the recipe. These soups will not curdle like sauces with milk and flour or cornstarch thickeners will.

◻ ◻ ◻

Processed cheese is the best type of cheese to use in a slow-cooker. Natural unprocessed cheese will separate, and the solids will become hard.

◻ ◻ ◻

When roasting a stuffed chicken in a slow-cooker, **reduce the amount of liquid** called for in the stuffing recipe.

◻ ◻ ◻

To **adapt your own favorite recipes** to slow-cooker cooking, reduce the liquid and seasonings called for. Long, slow, covered cooking creates condensation and intensifies the flavors of all seasonings, including salt and pepper. Start by reducing the liquid and the seasonings by one-third. After you have made the recipe once, adjust the quantities of these ingredients to suit your taste. Many variables contribute to how much you should reduce liquid and seasonings: the size of the cooker, the make (manufacturer) of the cooker, the amount of starch in the recipe, and the style of cover on the cooker. (Lightweight plastic covers on some cookers are raised slightly by the buildup of steam within the cooker, and some moisture escapes. Cookers with heavy glass or metal covers will hold more moisture in.)

◻ ◻ ◻

To **adapt the cooking times** of your favorite recipes to a slow-cooker, multiply the cooking time by 5 or 6 for the low setting and 3 or 4 for the high setting. Note any changes you have made on your recipe for future reference.

◻ ◻ ◻

If your slow-cooker has low and high settings only and you want to find out what temperatures those settings indicate, fill your pot with water, turn the setting to low and **test the water with a candy thermometer** after 2 hours. Then turn the setting up to high and test in another 2 hours. Temperature settings lower than 200° F are only for keeping cooked foods warm, not for cooking.

TOOLS OF THE TRADE 21

At a temperature lower than 200° F you risk not only spoilage, but also the development of harmful bacteria.

□ □ □

Vegetables cooked in a slow-cooker take as much as 4 hours longer than meat. That is why stew recipes take so long to cook and why most slow-cooker manufacturers suggest that you **put the vegetables beneath the meat.** I go even further and suggest that you **parboil vegetables** in a small amount of water or broth or **sauté them** in a small amount of fat before adding them to the bottom of the pot. Use the cooking juices or fat called for in the recipe. This will shorten cooking time and prevent the undercooked taste and ing texture of vegetables in slow-cooker recipes.

□ □ □

To eliminate too much moisture in the slow-cooker when baking casseroles, potatoes, or oven-type roasts, **cover the top** of the slow-cooker with 3–4 layers of paper towels before putting the cover snugly in place.

□ □ □

Whenever a slow-cooker recipe recommends cooking for 6–8 or 8–10 hours, the wide range indicates that the product will usually be done in the minimum time and will hold, maintaining its quality, for the maximum time.

Microwave Ovens

Follow the manufacturer's instructions for using your microwave oven — he knows his product better than anyone. Turn and stir as directed. Stirring is important in microwave cooking because it equalizes the temperatures within the dish.

□ □ □

When a microwave recipe gives a range of times, such as 4–6 minutes, always **test at the minimum time** to see how much more time is needed. Once food is overcooked, there's nothing you can do about it.

□ □ □

Follow the manufacturer's directions for standing time. Keep in mind that food cooked in a microwave oven continues to cook for several minutes after the oven is shut off, so **undercook slightly** while you are getting used to the timing of your oven. You can always return the food to the oven for a few more minutes if necessary.

□ □ □

Moisture does not evaporate easily in a microwave oven. Water is driven to the surface of the food where it will evaporate slightly, but not enough to crisp toppings, crusts, or skin on poultry.

□ □ □

For crisp toppings on microwave-cooked dishes, **add toppings after the food is cooked** and crisp them under the broiler.

□ □ □

To make the most of microwave-cooking speed and still get oven-baked taste and texture, cook casseroles and roasts in a microwave until they are **two-thirds done,** then transfer the dish to a preheated conventional oven. Finish baking for approximately one-third of the total cooking time suggested in the recipe.

□ □ □

Potatoes can be completely baked in a microwave oven, then transferred to a *cold* conventional oven to improve the texture. Set the oven temperature at 450° F and bake the potatoes for 10 minutes. They will crisp on the outside and dry out somewhat on the inside, making them nice and fluffy without being overbaked.

□ □ □

To **adapt your favorite recipes** to microwave cooking, reduce the liquid by one-fourth and the seasonings by one-third. Less moisture is required and seasonings tend to be intensified in microwave cooking. After making the recipe once, adjust the quantities of liquid and seasonings, if necessary, to suit your taste. Make sure to note any changes on your recipes.

□ □ □

In microwave cooking, the fat is drawn to the surface of a roast, where it browns slightly on a roast cooked for a long time. However, **prebrowning in a heavy skillet** gives a better appearance. I do not like the browning agents sold for this purpose because of the high sodium content in most of them. They also change the taste of the food.

□ □ □

Sugar attracts microwave energy. A Danish roll with a jam filling will become *very* hot in the center in seconds, while the outer area of the roll remains somewhat cool. This has caused some rather bad burns for unsuspecting people.

□ □ □

Small pieces of meat cook faster than large pieces of meat in any kind of cooking, and this is especially true in microwave cooking. Thin pieces, such as chicken wings and backs, cook faster than thick pieces, such as breasts and legs, and should be placed in the **center of the baking dish,** with the thicker portions **at the edge.**

TOOLS OF THE TRADE

In microwave cookery, **bone conducts heat.** The piece of meat nearest the bone cooks first. Boneless cuts cook less rapidly, but more evenly.

Fat distribution is important in meats that are microwaved. Evenly distributed fat (marbleized meat) tenderizes and helps to cook the meat evenly. Large fatty areas attract the microwaves away from the meat, slowing cooking.

When cooking vegetables in a microwave oven, **add a minimum of water,** whether the vegetables are fresh or frozen. Extra water slows cooking. (However, foods with a low moisture content, such as parboiled dried beans, do not cook well in a microwave oven.)

When **doubling** the size of a recipe, **increase the microwave cooking time by half** and check for doneness at that time.

Dense, heavy foods take longer to microwave than porous, airy foods. For instance, a brownie takes longer to cook than a large bundt cake in spite of the fact that it is smaller. Solid pieces of meat are more dense than ground meat, and baked potatoes are more dense than mashed potatoes.

Use only **microwave-safe dishes** in microwave ovens. Foods that need only brief cooking can be cooked or reheated on paper plates or paper towels.

Covered casseroles cook faster in both microwave and conventional ovens because steam is held in.

Shallow, round, straight-sided dishes are better for microwave cooking than deep, rectangular or square dishes.

Casserole dishes **without covers** can go in a microwave covered tightly with a good quality plastic wrap. **Dry paper towels** can be used where tight covering is not necessary — to prevent spattering, for example.

Wax paper forms a loose cover similar to partial covering.

To **tenderize meats** and prevent dryness from microwave ovens, cook meat in cooking bags. Do not use metal ties — tie the bags with string. Follow the directions carefully for using these bags.

□ □ □

Place a piece of paper towel between the oven floor and breads or rolls that are being reheated in a microwave oven. This will **prevent wet bottoms.**

□ □ □

To **steam fish in a microwave oven,** cover the baking dish with a couple of layers of damp paper towels. One pound fish fillets may be steamed in a microwave on high power for 5½–8 minutes (depending on thickness of fillets) or 11–14 minutes on medium power.

□ □ □

When microwaving **dense foods** such as meat loaf or cake, use bundt pans or ring molds with raised centers. These pans conduct heat more evenly.

□ □ □

Freeze leftover mashed potatoes, mashed sweet potatoes, and bread stuffing in ½-cup servings by forming them into balls and tray-freezing until solid. Pack loosely in plastic bags. To **reheat** in a microwave, place on a microwave-safe dinner plate with frozen meat or fish and vegetables. Microwave uncovered on high for 4–5 minutes. Cover lightly and finish heating through on medium (4–6 minutes).

□ □ □

For a **quick cheese sauce,** place a slice of cheddar cheese over a serving of cooked vegetables. Microwave on high for 45 seconds to melt the cheese.

□ □ □

Peel chestnuts quickly and easily in a microwave oven. Place chestnuts on a plate and microwave them on high; turn them halfway through the cooking time. Slip off the skins when the nuts are cool enough to handle. One chestnut takes about 5 seconds; twelve take 1 minute.

TOOLS OF THE TRADE 25

CHAPTER 2
TIPS FOR SMART COOKS

There are tricks to every trade, and in this chapter I am going to share with you my secrets for making life easier in the kitchen. Reread this chapter often until you have memorized those suggestions that are most helpful to you.

Shopping

Add staples to your **grocery list** as soon as you open the last bag, box, or jar. Otherwise, you may come up short when you are your busiest.

☐ ☐ ☐

Clean out the refrigerator and organize the freezer before going shopping — it saves confusion when you get home.

☐ ☐ ☐

When doing large-scale shopping in hot weather, **bring a cooler** in the car to keep perishables cold until you get home.

☐ ☐ ☐

Take **older family members** shopping with you. Show them the layout of the store and explain unit pricing; then let them take turns doing the shopping to free you for cooking chores.

☐ ☐ ☐

Fruits and vegetables wrapped in plastic look pretty, but they can be costly to the buyer. The wrapping process itself sometimes bruises the product, and the continued pressure of the plastic wrap speeds deterioration. Buy only the **freshest, unwrapped fruits and vegetables.** Make sure they are free of blemishes, and buy only what you need.

☐ ☐ ☐

When buying frozen fruits and vegetables, buy the **large bags of loose-pack products** so that you can take out only what you need.

☐ ☐ ☐

It's worth the extra pennies to **have chicken cut** at the store, unless you are an expert. The time saved will be worth more than the few pennies spent.

□ □ □

Boned and rolled roasts cook better in microwave ovens and slow-cookers than meat with a bone, but buying lean roasts **with the bones in** and asking the butcher to bone them for you is a better idea. Ask to keep the bones and cook them along with the meat for better flavored pan juices and richer gravies.

□ □ □

When buying large, wrapped roasts, ask the butcher to let you **see the roast unwrapped.** There's no need to waste money on chunks of fat hidden on the underside.

Cooking

To determine the **size of your baking dishes,** measure the outside of the bottom of the dish, not the top (with the exception of pie plates). Tops flare out slightly even in most straight-sided dishes and give misleading dimensions.

□ □ □

Always **work from right to left** or vice versa when adding seasonings and ingredients to a recipe. This will prevent mistakes when you have interruptions.

□ □ □

Rich-tasting broths are essential to the flavor of good soups and sauces. When making homemade broths be sure to reduce them enough to produce a rich flavor; otherwise, add bouillon powder (cubes are too salty) to enrich the flavor.

□ □ □

To make rich-tasting broth from **bouillon powder,** add 1½ teaspoons powder to 1 cup water for each cup of broth called for in the recipe.

□ □ □

Soups and stews prepared **one or more days before serving** taste much better. Flavors have an opportunity to blend.

□ □ □

Many times when soup or stew recipes call for **browning the meat** before adding the liquid, it is only for appearance's sake — it has nothing to do with the flavor or texture of the finished product. You can save time by skipping this step.

□ □ □

Make delicious **meat pies** by topping heated leftover stews with leftover mashed potatoes or baking powder biscuits and baking in a 375° F oven for 20–25 minutes.

□ □ □

To **prevent fish cooking odors,** fish can be sealed in a boilable freezer bag and cooked by immersing the bag in boiling water for just a few minutes (depending on the size of the fish).

□ □ □

The secret to **successful stir-fry dishes** is not to crowd too much into the wok or skillet at one time. Moisture from the vegetables must be allowed to evaporate in order for the vegetables to cook tender crisp without steaming. When doubling a recipe, use two large skillets instead of one.

□ □ □

Cream soups can make **quick sauces.** For beef and veal, try cream of mushroom soup; for bland vegetables, fish, and lamb, cream of celery soup; for chicken, turkey, veal, and lamb, cream of chicken soup; and for fish, cream of shrimp or cream of chicken soup.

□ □ □

Tofu may be substituted for meat in pasta sauces and stir-fried dishes, as well as for the ground beef in any casserole.

□ □ □

For extra nutrition bind meat loaf and meatballs with **oatmeal** instead of bread or cracker crumbs. Use ¼ cup uncooked oatmeal for each ½ cup of soft breadcrumbs called for in the recipe. Use ¼ cup of oatmeal for each ¼ cup of dry breadcrumbs or cracker crumbs called for.

□ □ □

When cooking rice or pasta ahead of time, or potatoes for hash browns or creamed potatoes, **undercook** them. They should be cooked but still slightly firm when done. Cool them quickly to prevent further cooking. They will finish cooking when reheated or used in casseroles.

□ □ □

For **light and fluffy mashed potatoes,** add ¼ teaspoon baking powder per pound of potatoes while mashing. Potatoes just dug in the summer or early fall have a higher moisture content than potatoes that are winter stored, so go easy when adding milk for mashed potatoes. Winter-stored potatoes have lost a large percentage of their moisture and have become starchier. Because of this, they make better mashed potatoes and fluffier baked potatoes.

□ □ □

Before cooking, cut the root end *out* of **winter-stored onions** to eliminate the too strong taste often associated with them.

□ □ □

Let old onions sprout. Use the green tops as scallions in stir-fry dishes and salads.

□ □ □

To **peel fresh garlic**, press the side of a clove with a wide-blade knife — the peel will split and come off easily.

□ □ □

Outer leaves of lettuce make a great addition to soups and stir-fried dishes. When cooked, lettuce is actually a sweet-tasting vegetable, and the outer leaves are the most nutritious. Before using, wash these outer leaves carefully to remove spoilage-retardant sprays.

□ □ □

Scrub vegetables thoroughly before peeling. Use the **clean peelings** to make excellent-tasting and nutritious soup stocks.

□ □ □

Regardless of how large your food processor bowl is, **never fill it more than one-third full** when chopping vegetables. Otherwise, some will be overchopped before all are finished. Always cut vegetables into uniform-size chunks and do not crowd them in the bowl.

□ □ □

Quiche and custard pie fillings can be baked **without a crust**. Spray a pie plate with vegetable oil, pour in the filling mixture and bake (see recipe, p. 109).

□ □ □

Quiche and custard pie fillings can be prepared **three or four days ahead of time** and refrigerated until needed, or they can be frozen for up to three months. Shake the fillings well before pouring them into a crust.

□ □ □

Pie crust for quiches and custard pies can also be prepared and frozen ahead of time. To bake, defrost the filling, shake it well, and pour it into the frozen crust. Bake as usual.

□ □ □

Frozen rolls need ten to twelve minutes to defrost and reheat in the oven at 400° F; fresh rolls need only five to seven minutes, depending on size. Place the rolls in a paper bag, run the bag under cold water until the bag is wet (not sopping) all over, and place it in the oven. The steam created by the water will fluff the rolls up on the insides and crisp them on the outside.

□ □ □

To remove breads steamed in cans, open the bottom and push the bread through.

□ □ □

Make homemade bread dough before you start dinner at night. The extra heat in the kitchen will **help the bread to rise faster,** and the bread will be ready to bake after dinner.

□ □ □

If you are baking more than one loaf of yeast or quick-rising bread at one time, **use a scale to weigh the pans of bread** as soon as you fill them, and make sure that they are about equal. This will ensure equal baking time.

□ □ □

When you prepare recipes calling for dry and wet ingredients, and you are using an electric mixer or mixing by hand, you usually mix all the liquid ingredients in the mixing bowl and then slowly add the dry ingredients. To prepare mixes with a food processor, **you reverse this procedure.** You put the dry ingredients in the processor bowl, and with the processor going, you slowly add the wet ingredients.

□ □ □

Recipes in this book that call for the use of a food processor can be made **with a mixer or by hand** by simply reversing the above process.

□ □ □

When making yeast breads and pie crusts in a food processor, keep in mind that these appliances work so fast that the dough does not have time to absorb all the moisture called for in the recipe, so your dough **should look and feel slightly stickier** than it would if you were making it any other way. If you add more flour to compensate, your pie crusts will be dry and fall apart when you roll them out, and your breads will be heavy.

□ □ □

In humid weather, yeast doughs do not absorb as much moisture. **Go easy when adding liquid** to food processor doughs, and doughs made with a mixer or by hand may need a little extra flour.

□ □ □

Never beat eggs when adding them to a food processor.

□ □ □

When you roll out yeast doughs or homemade pasta, the gluten strands in the dough are going to give you resistance. To overcome this and be able to roll the dough as thin as you want to, **let the dough rest for a minute** when it starts to spring back. This will ease the resistance, and you will be able to roll out the dough as thin as you want. With large pieces of dough it may be necessary to do this two or three times.

□ □ □

Contrary to what most recipe directions say, I think that yeast breads rise more evenly and have a finer grained texture if they are started in a **cold oven.** Hot ovens tend to make these doughs puff, which creates large air pockets. Starting breads in a cold oven saves energy, too.

□ □ □

The temperature of the room is very important to the rising of yeast doughs. A temperature of 72° F or warmer is ideal. If your home is colder, you can overcome the problem by setting dough to rise in a **gas oven** with a pilot light, near a **wood stove,** on the top of a **self-defrosting refrigerator,** in the **oven** with a bowl of boiling water on the bottom shelf, or in a **dishwasher** preheated as if to warm plates, and then turned off.

□ □ □

When setting yeast breads to rise, **cover the entire bowl** with a towel. This will keep the warmth in better than if the sides are exposed to cooler temperatures. Use only lightweight towels; heavy towels will inhibit rising.

□ □ □

To **crisp cream puffs,** put them on a wire cooling rack, place the rack on a cookie sheet, and put it in a cold oven. Turn the oven to 200° F and time it for 3 minutes. Turn off the oven, and let the puffs remain in the unopened oven for 10 minutes.

□ □ □

Homemade or commercially prepared fruit jellies and preserves thinned with a little water make wonderful **toppings** for ice cream and cheesecake, as well as quick glazes for meat, fish, and poultry.

□ □ □

To **crush ice** without an ice crusher, place it in a plastic bag or cloth dish towel and hit it with a hammer.

□ □ □

Keep canned peaches and refrigerated *Fruit Crisp Topping* (p. 65) on hand for quick desserts. Or make a few large chocolate chip cookies, sandwich a slice of ice cream between, wrap and freeze for quick desserts.

Keeping Food

Make sure that **spices and herbs** are fresh. Ground spices and herbs will stay fresh for six months, whole spices for a year after they are opened. To ensure that you are always cooking with fresh herbs, date the container when you first open it.

□ □ □

Keep **hard natural cheese** in a covered container in a cool place (but not in the refrigerator). Add a few cubes of sugar to the container to prevent mold. If some mold has already formed on your cheese, place the cheese in a covered container with sugar, and the mold will disappear. Natural cheese is best served at room temperature.

□ □ □

Eggs boiled in the shell must be refrigerated promptly. Otherwise, airborne bacteria will enter the shell and could cause serious illness. This is especially true in warm weather.

□ □ □

Take five minutes some evening to chop a full pound of **walnuts** for baking. This will save two to three minutes every time you use a recipe calling for nuts. Store the nuts in a tightly covered container. They may be frozen for an indefinite period or left at room temperature for use within two months.

□ □ □

Save **fresh celery leaves**. Dry them on a cookie sheet or in a paper bag with holes punched in it in a warm, dry place. Use them in soups and stews — they are much more flavorful than the purchased dried celery flakes.

□ □ □

To keep a large, thick, sweet, slicing **onion** at its best for salads and hamburgers, peel the onion the first time you cut into it, leaving the root end (roots and all) attached. Place the unused portion in a ziptop plastic bag, press out the excess air, and refrigerate. It will keep well right down to the end.

□ □ □

With the exception of lettuce, **vegetables** prepared in advance for salads should be refrigerated in plastic ziptop bags that are not completely closed. A one-inch opening allows vegetables to breathe, so they do not become mushy. **Lettuce** can be sealed in a bag or container.

□ □ □

Buy **fresh parsley** in bunches, rinse and drain well, and freeze in food-safe plastic bags. To use, remove from the freezer and chop off what you need while it's still frozen. Return the unused portion to the freezer.

□ □ □

If you do not have a freezer or are short of freezer space, **reduce homemade soup stock** to one-fourth its volume and store it in the refrigerator. If it has not been used up in a month, bring it to a boil on top of the stove and refrigerate it again. It will keep indefinitely. To reconstitute, combine 1 part jellied stock with 3 parts water. Use for soups, gravies, and sauces.

CHAPTER 3
CHAIN COOKING

Chain cooking is my term for preparing foods in advance for more than one meal at a time. To start with, I suggest preparation of vegetables, soup stocks, sauces, and mixes for baked goods. These basics can be combined with other ingredients over a period of a week or longer to prepare many different recipes quickly and easily. This method of cooking saves time and adds tremendous variety to meal planning. As the chain-cooking cook becomes more experienced, meals can be prepared almost entirely ahead of time. Chain cooking can cut the amount of time you spend in the kitchen almost in half — certainly by a third.

Plan to start your chain-cooking weekends by making up all the basic mixes you want to have on hand (see page 61). These mixes will save you hours of cooking time and give you a multitude of quick and easy recipes. Choose another weekend to dice, slice, and chop vegetables and cheese for tray freezing; a weekend for putting together soups, stews, and casseroles (using the vegetables you have prepared ahead of time); and maybe one weekend for breads, rolls, and desserts. You can go on with an endless variety of combinations, becoming more experienced and confident with the system and gradually completing more and more of the week's cooking in advance.

This method of food preparation often puts the cart before the horse. You will come home to a dinner that takes just minutes to prepare. After dinner, using foods that are already prepared (or sometimes using leftovers), you might spend a few minutes putting together a casserole that you will only have to slip into the oven when you come home the following evening. Other times you might prepare a casserole in your slow-cooker to be refrigerated overnight and started the next morning. It will be ready when you come home at night. Add a salad, a beverage, and a light dessert, and you'll have dinner on the table in ten minutes. Many casseroles can be prepared a day in advance and refrigerated until baking time.

Do you have most of your energy early in the day, or do you just start to get revved up around four in the afternoon? Make the most of your energy by using your best time of day to do chain cooking. If you work when you feel your best, you will accomplish twice as much in half the time.

You won't be able to whiz through the first few cooking sessions as quickly as I do. The first week or two can even be somewhat confusing and tiring. But after you have worked your way through two or three weekends, your mastery of these techniques will make it possible for you to make up your own menu, work out your shopping list, set up your weekend work program using your own favorite recipes, and get through your weekend cooking in a snap.

Try the menu plan on page 40 some week, then work out your own, using similar types of recipes at first, so that you can use the same time-saving techniques until you get used to cooking this way.

You might want to try chain cooking with a friend — each would pay half the cost and split the food. You could chain cook one day at your house and another at your friend's, so that the use of staples would be fairly divided.

I should repeat that you must prepare your mixes in advance of making the recipes, in order for this system to be most effective.

The Basic Steps

This chapter presents the basic steps in chain-cooking on page 39. Grouped together, they give the appearance of a great deal of work. However, if you follow my suggestions, you will find everything falling into place with surprising ease. For instance, if you feel that spending half an hour preparing menus for the week to come is too much time, ask yourself how much time you spend each day trying to figure out what you are going to feed your family for dinner. Often a quick trip to the store is necessary for even the simplest meal. Menu planning and shopping from a menu plan save untold hours all by themselves.

As you become accustomed to menu planning and shopping for groceries with a list based on a menu, you can cut your major shopping trips to twice a month and, eventually, to only once a month. Although this does require more storage space, it saves tremendous amounts of time. Just one quick stop per week for fresh foods and dairy products takes care of my needs in a matter of minutes.

There is going to be a surplus in your freezer, however, and eventually you will have a large variety of foods on hand. At this point, you will have to determine how often you need to do chain cooking to keep ahead. The costs will not only level off, you will also be saving money on your grocery budget — while probably eating better than ever before.

Plan your menus in the evening when you are relaxing with your family — get their ideas when possible. It shouldn't take more than half an hour. Make out your grocery list the night before you shop, checking newspaper ads for specials. The following guide should help you to get through the list quickly.

☐ List all categories of groceries as headings on a sheet of paper, see p. 42.

☐ Using your menu plan, take out all the recipes you will be using in the coming week. List all the ingredients that you need under the proper headings.

☐ Go over your menu again and list all needed items not included in the recipes: salad ingredients, beverages, etc. Include breakfast and lunch foods and snacks.

☐ Keep a small notebook in the kitchen to list items as you run out. Add to your grocery list any items from this list that have not already been included.

☐ Go over the Pantry Staples (p. 177) for items you should always have on hand.

☐ If you are going to prepare any recipe in quantity, make sure to note on your grocery list exactly how much of each ingredient you need. You can't make four meat loaves with one and a half pounds of ground beef. (Also make a note on your recipe of how many times you are multiplying the ingredients. This will help you remember to add the proper amount of each.)

Make a list of all the recipes you would like to prepare on chain-cooking day, then make a work plan first thing in the morning (or the night before), using my plan (page 39) as a guide. Follow through with your work plan as closely as possible. Get family help with peeling and chopping vegetables and packaging food whenever possible.

Double up on soups, sauces, meat loaves, and casseroles. It takes only a few minutes longer to cook two or three batches than it does just one. Pencil in the changes right on your recipe, so you won't forget to add the right amount of any ingredient.

If you have a small kitchen, outsize pans and bowls used for quantity cooking can be stored in cardboard boxes or plastic laundry baskets in any convenient closet. Small paring knives, measuring spoons, spatulas, wooden spoons, wire whisks, peelers, and corers can be stored in a shoe bag on the back of any convenient door. Use a little imagination to give yourself extra space. Pots, pans, and large bowls that you will need do not have to be placed right where you are working. They can be temporarily put on chairs, the top of the washer, a card table, or even an ironing board. These same areas can be used to hold the staple foods you will be cooking with. The main idea is to get everything out where it is handy and you won't have to waste time looking for it.

If refrigeration is a problem when preparing foods for several days, invest in a large picnic cooler to store fresh vegetables, sauces, and small items. I make ice bags (p. 15), or I fill several milk cartons with water and freeze them. In the early part of the week when I have many foods on hand, I store some items in the cooler with the ice packs, replacing the ice each evening — it takes only minutes to do. A small, secondhand refrigerator (often available for as little as $35) also can be of immense help.

Allow yourself plenty of time, so you won't have to rush. As you get more familiar with this type of cooking, the time you spend in the kitchen will be reduced dramatically. Read all recipes through at least once before starting — this will prevent mistakes.

When your cooking chores are finished for the day, use my daily menu plans (pp. 180–181) as a guide and jot down some notes on the order in which you would like to prepare meals for the coming week. Meal plans can always be changed at the last minute, but having the line-up already planned frees you mentally from having to make these decisions on a daily basis. You will be amazed at the lift this small freedom gives you.

Remember: It is *not* necessary to prepare everything I have listed here. However, it *is* important to the time-saving element of this book to prepare in advance such things as basic mixes, vegetables and cheese, salad dressings, soup stocks, and sauces. When you have time, include brown-and-serve bread or rolls.

Basic Steps in Chain Cooking

Following are the basic steps in chain cooking. On pp. 40–51, I will show you how to implement these steps according to a sample week's menu and chain-cooking work plan. Steps 7 to 9 serve only as a rough outline of what has to be done in what order. The specific tasks vary according to the menu being prepared. This outline should help you put together a work plan for your own weekly menus.

Step 1

Plan your menu for the week.

Step 2

Prepare your shopping list.

Step 3

Shop.

Step 4

Write out your plan of action for chain cooking day, using the plan on p. 40 as a guide. Check your recipes carefully; line up those that require long cooking for early in the day.

Step 5

Assemble all the recipe ingredients before you start to cook.

Step 6

Assemble all the equipment you will need.

Step 7

Preliminary food preparation. Peel, chop, slice, dice, or shred all the ingredients that need it (vegetables, cheese, etc.).

Step 8

Intermediate food preparation. One at a time, assemble combination foods (casseroles, soups, etc. — anything that must be "put together"). Start with the dishes that must cook longest.

Step 9

Finishing food preparation. Cook any foods that can be cooked in advance.

Step 10

Package all food in meal-size or single-serving containers (depending on how they will be most useful). Label and date all containers, list the contents in your record of foods on hand, and store them in the refrigerator or freezer.

Step 11

Clean up and relax!

Step 1
Plan Your Menu

These menus were planned for a family of four. Starred items can be all or partially prepared on chain-cooking day. A dagger indicates commercially packaged products. Add to each meal your favorite breads or rolls and a beverage of choice.

Saturday

Scalloped Potatoes*
Baked Ham with Pineapple*
Fresh vegetable salad*
Ice cream †

□ □ □

Sunday

Meat Loaf*
Mashed Potatoes*
Cabbage, Carrot, and Raisin Salad*
Strawberry Pie

Monday

Crustless Broccoli Quiche*
Fresh vegetable salad*
Leftover pie from Sunday

□ □ □

Tuesday

Stir-Fried Chicken and Vegetables*
Brown rice*
24-Hour Salad*
Fresh fruit of choice

Wednesday

Vermicelli with
Quick-and-Easy Pasta Sauce*
Buttered corn †
Cucumbers in sour cream †
Ice Cream †

Thursday

Fried Chicken*
Buttered egg noodles †
Steamed carrots*
Cabbage salad*
Peach Shortcake

Friday

Stir-Fried Beef with Snowpeas*
Brown rice*
Fresh vegetable salad*
Quick-and-Easy Chocolate Cake with whipped topping

Step 2
Prepare Your Shopping List

This sample shopping list includes *everything* for the menu plan on page 40. You may have many of these ingredients on hand already, or you may wish to omit certain items in the menu plan. I have given quantities wherever possible; however, the quantities of some products, such as the fresh produce, will depend on how often those products will be used for lunches, snacks, etc., as well as dinners.

Step 3
Shop

Your shopping list is complete, and you should be able to shop for the week in 45 to 60 minutes on your way home from work. Your shopping list identifies your needs clearly so that you don't have to stop and think about what you need.

Step 4
Write Out Your Plan of Action

Follow the guideline in the coming pages to make up your own work plan. Once you start working, try to relax. Work slowly and carefully. The first few weeks it will take you longer to accomplish all that you have set out for yourself because you have to take time to read directions carefully, but within a very short time, you will find that just a glance at your work plan will be enough to get you to the next step. Time and experience will cut your work time in half. Pace yourself so that you won't get exhausted. It helps to turn on your favorite music while you work.

All prepared foods should be refrigerated or frozen as soon as they are cooled enough. Most food that needs to be frozen can be refrigerated until all the work is completed. This will save time and prevent the loss of cold air that results when a freezer is opened too often.

This work plan includes soups and sandwich fillings for lunches. If your family doesn't eat lunch at home or take it with them, you will not need to make these items unless you want them for weekend meals. Simply go over the work plan and cross off the steps pertaining to these items.

SHOPPING LIST

Fresh Produce

10-12 medium to large potatoes
1 pint fresh strawberries
4 pounds onions
assorted fresh fruit
2 pounds cabbage
2 pounds carrots
lettuce
spinach
cucumbers
fresh ginger
4 green peppers
1 red pepper
1 bunch celery
radishes
mushrooms (optional)

Meats and Fish

7 pounds lean ground beef
2 pounds boneless top round steak
10 pounds frying chicken, cut in pieces
2–3 pound precooked ham

Pasta and Rice

8 ounces fine noodles
8 ounces medium egg noodles
8 ounces vermicelli
1 pound brown rice

Dairy Foods

6 ounces cheddar cheese
8 ounces sour cream
16 ounces ricotta cheese
4 ounces blue cheese
8 ounces all-purpose cream
2 dozen eggs
milk
butter or margarine
8 ounces Swiss cheese
8 ounces grated Parmesan cheese
½ pint whipping cream (optional)

Baking Goods

4 ounces unsweetened cocoa
2 pounds whole wheat flour
1 pound honey
3 pounds vegetable shortening
1 pound raisins
1 prepared graham cracker crumb crust
1 6-ounce package strawberry flavored gelatin
5 pounds sugar
10 pounds all-purpose unbleached flour
2 pounds brown sugar

Dry Goods

paper towels
freezer labels
marking pen
freezer bags
freezer containers
tin foil
wax paper
plastic wrap

Frozen Foods

½ gallon ice cream
2 frozen pie crusts
8 ounces frozen peas
20 ounces frozen broccoli
10 ounces frozen cauliflower
8 ounces frozen whipped topping
12 ounces frozen snowpeas
16 ounces whole-kernel corn

Baked Goods

1 loaf French bread
1 loaf whole wheat or white bread
12 hard rolls

SHOPPING LIST, cont.

Condiments
ketchup
mustard
mayonnaise
salad dressing
sweet pickle relish
2 packages milk-and-mayonnaise-type dressing mix powder (1 buttermilk, 1 creamy Italian)
vegetable oil
vinegar
Worcestershire sauce
soy sauce
cooking sherry
vegetable oil spray (e.g., Pam)

Seasonings
celery flakes
dried basil
crushed red pepper
dried chives
Italian seasoning
onion powder
garlic powder
poultry seasoning
salt
pepper
dried sweet marjoram
thyme
dried mustard
paprika
dried parsley
cayenne

Canned Fruits and Juices
8 ounces pineapple chunks canned in juice
16-ounce can sliced peaches
8 ounces lemon juice

Miscellaneous
1 10¾-ounce can cream of celery soup
5 15-ounce cans chicken broth
1 15-ounce can beef broth
1 jar chicken bouillon powder
2 ounces slivered almonds
1 package quick-cooking oatmeal
24 ounces tomato paste

Step 5
Assemble All the Recipe Ingredients

This work plan includes partial or complete preparation of the following dishes for a family of four:

☐ Scalloped potatoes for Saturday

☐ Meat Loaf for Sunday and one extra meal

☐ Peeled whole potatoes for Sunday

☐ Cabbage and carrots for cabbage salad on Monday and Tuesday

☐ Egg mixture for Broccoli Quiche for Monday, plus one to freeze

☐ Chicken for Stir-Fried Chicken with Vegetables on Tuesday

☐ Brown rice to reheat for Tuesday and Friday, plus some to freeze

☐ Quick-and-Easy Pasta Sauce for Wednesday, plus three meals to freeze

☐ Fried Chicken for Thursday, plus three meals to freeze

☐ Whole peeled carrots for Tuesday

☐ Beef for Stir-Fried Beef with Snowpeas on Friday, plus one meal to freeze

☐ Broccoli, Cauliflower, and Cheddar Soup for lunches

☐ Chicken Vegetable Soup for lunches

☐ Ham salad and egg salad for sandwich fillings (each filling makes enough for six to eight sandwiches)

☐ Vegetables for salads (your choice)

ORGANIZE YOUR KITCHEN: FOOD

The following items should be assembled near your work center:

8 cups chicken broth
24 ounces tomato paste
mayonnaise
dried parsley
garlic powder
prepared mustard
crushed red pepper
quick-cooking oatmeal
fine noodles
1 can cream of celery soup
onion powder
poultry seasoning
dried chives
Worcestershire sauce
vegetable oil
sweet pickle relish
2 dozen eggs

honey
salt
pepper
cayenne
dried basil
milk-and-mayonnaise dressing mix powder
chicken bouillon powder
brown rice
Parmesan cheese
lemon juice

By the sink, place the following vegetables:

potatoes   onions
carrots   celery
green and red peppers
lettuce, spinach, and any other vegetables that you want to prepare for the week
cabbage

This group should remain in their containers in the refrigerator (or picnic cooler):

frozen broccoli
frozen cauliflower
butter or margarine
milk
cream
ricotta cheese
cheddar cheese
ground beef
precooked ham
chicken pieces
round steak

Step 6
Assemble All Equipment

Before starting to cook, arrange your work space to maximize kitchen efficiency.

ORGANIZE YOUR KITCHEN: EQUIPMENT

In the most convenient work area, set up the following:

food processor with chopping, slicing, and shredding blades
blender
chopping board
sharp knives
kitchen scale
several medium-size bowls to hold processed vegetables, meat, and eggs
2–3 small timers (timer on stove or microwave can also be used)

Next to the sink, place:

vegetable scrub brush
vegetable peeler
colander
sharp paring knife

Next to the stove, place:

measuring cups (liquid and dry measure)
measuring spoons
large spoons (wooden and slotted)
small saucepan
2–3 large covered saucepans
8-quart covered saucepan
covered soup kettle (large enough for 10 pounds of chicken and water)
2 meat loaf pans or 2 12-cup muffin tins
large heavy skillet or electric fry pan
deep-fat thermometer (if not using electric fry pan)
paper towels
pot holders
vegetable oil spray

In a convenient place for packaging food later, place:

wire cooling racks
2–3 large cookie sheets for tray-freezing
plastic freezer bags or boxes
large assortment of refrigerator containers
ziptop plastic bags
freezer labels
indelible marking pen
notebook and pen

Step 7
Preliminary Food Preparation

The menu and recipes in this work plan are based on serving a family of four and assume that you're chain cooking on a Saturday. Several of these recipes have been doubled or quadrupled to make the most of chain cooking. If you don't want to make these recipes in quantity, skip the instructions in this section and refer to the original recipes in Part 2.

Read the entire step-by-step plan before you begin. Some of the recipes require a mix to be made in advance (see "Homemade Mixes", page 61).

The timers will help you keep your place. To avoid confusion, mark each timer with a small slip of paper that tells you which food it is timing.

Label every food you place in the freezer and refrigerator and list it in a small notebook. Cross off items as they are used; you will find yourself wasting much less food with this system.

If you are going to skip a recipe or make a different quantity, make a note of what changes you are making in the work plan. Be careful to omit only those steps that apply to the change you are making in the plan.

When you have familiarized yourself with the rest of the plan, begin.

1. Fill the sink with hot sudsy water for quick rinse-offs. (The processor bowl and chopping blade should be rinsed after each item is chopped.)

2. Put 6 eggs in cold water and bring it to a boil. Reduce the heat and simmer, uncovered, for 8 minutes. SET A TIMER. Drain and set aside to cool.

3. Wrap 2 whole chicken breasts and put them in the freezer for 1 hour. It's easier to bone partially frozen chicken.

4. Put the remaining chicken in the large soup kettle. Cover it with 10–12 cups water and add 3 tablespoons of chicken bouillon powder. Cover and bring to a boil. Reduce the heat and simmer for 10 minutes. SET A TIMER. Do not overcook. When done, turn off the heat and let the chicken cool in the broth.

5. Peel or trim as needed for the food processor:
   10–12 medium to large potatoes (then place in a bowl of cold water)
   2 pounds cabbage
   4 pounds onions
   4 large green peppers and 1 large red pepper
   1 bunch celery (leave the bunch whole; cut each rib in half lengthwise without separating them from the stalk; rinse thor-

oughly under cold running water)
1½ pounds carrots

6. Place the top round steak on a cookie sheet and put in the freezer for 1 hour. If partially frozen, it will slice more easily for the stir-fry.

7. Cook the brown rice. Put 4½ cups hot water in a 2-quart saucepan. Add 4 teaspoons chicken bouillon powder and 1 teaspoon onion powder. Cover the pan and bring the water to a boil. Add 1 pound rice and return the water to a boil. Reduce the heat and simmer for 45 minutes. SET A TIMER.

8. Open the canned ham, cut off ½ pound, and return the rest to the refrigerator for **Baked Ham with Pineapple.**

9. Shell the 6 hard-cooked eggs and set them aside.

10. Fit the food processor with the chopping blade and chop the following:
    4 ounces potato for **Broccoli, Cauliflower and Cheddar Soup** (set aside in a small bowl)
    2 pounds onions for soups, sandwich filling, meat loaf, and spaghetti sauce
    3 green peppers for soups and sautéing
    ½ pound ham for sandwich filling
    6 hard-boiled eggs for sandwich filling
    Refrigerate ham and hard-boiled eggs after chopping.

11. Fit the processor with the shredding blade and shred the following:
    6 ounces cheddar cheese for broccoli soup

12. Fit the processor with the thin-slice blade and slice the following:
    2 pounds cabbage for cabbage salad and soups
    1 large green pepper for salads and stir-fries
    1 large red pepper for salads and stir-fries
    2 pounds onions for scalloped potatoes, salads, and stir-fries
    4 large potatoes for scalloped potatoes
    1 bunch celery for salads, soups, and stir-fries. Fit the whole bunch of celery, tops down, in the chute, and slice the ribs. If the halved ribs are too large, cut them into quarters lengthwise; leave the bottom attached to make processing easier.

13. Place the food processor bowl and the blades in the hot sudsy water.

14. Wrap the remaining whole, peeled potatoes in paper towels and sprinkle with cold water. Place them in plastic ziptop bags, press out all the air, and seal tightly. Refrigerate for Sunday.

15. Wrap the whole, peeled carrots as you did the potatoes. Refrigerate for Thursday.

Step 8
Intermediate Food Preparation

1. Assemble *Scalloped Potatoes.*
   Layer half of the sliced potatoes and the equivalent of 1 large sliced onion in a 2-quart casserole dish sprayed with vegetable oil. Put 1 can cream of celery soup, 1/3 cup milk, and 1/3 cup ricotta cheese in a blender container. Add a sprinkling of pepper and blend until smooth. Pour half of this mixture over the potatoes and onions. Add the remaining sliced potatoes and top with the remaining soup mixture. Cover tightly and refrigerate.

2. Drain the chicken in a large colander placed over another pan to catch the juices. Strain the broth for the soups to be made next. Wrap the chicken in plastic wrap and refrigerate until needed for *Chicken Vegetable Soup* and *Fried Chicken.*

3. Assemble the soups.
   Broccoli, Cauliflower, Cheddar Soup: Put 4 cups chicken broth in a 3½-quart saucepan. Add 2 tablespoons butter or margarine, 1 teaspoon onion powder, 10 ounces frozen broccoli, 10 ounces frozen cauliflower, and the reserved 4 ounces of chopped potato. Cover the pan. Bring the soup to a boil, reduce the heat, and cook for 10 minutes. SET A TIMER.
   When the timer goes off, remove a few pieces of broccoli and cauliflower with a slotted spoon and set them aside to be added later for texture. Re-cover the pan and continue cooking for an additional 10 minutes. SET A TIMER.
   Combine 6 ounces cheddar cheese and ½ cup all-purpose cream in a blender container. Add half of the broccoli mixture from the saucepan (do not overfill the blender or you may get scalded). Blend until very smooth. Pour into a bowl with the reserved vegetable pieces. Blend the remaining broccoli mixture and combine with the first half. Stir well and set aside to cool. Rinse the blender container.
   Chicken Vegetable Soup: Put 4 cups chicken broth in a 3½-quart saucepan. Add 4 cups sliced or diced vegetables. (Be sure to include onions, carrots, celery, and cabbage; they are important to the flavor of this soup.) Add 1 tablespoon butter or margarine, ½ teaspoon dried parsley, and 1/8 teaspoon poultry seasoning. Cover the pan. Bring the soup to a boil, reduce the heat, and simmer for 15 minutes. SET A TIMER.
   Dice 1 cup of cooked chicken (from the refrigerator). When the timer goes off, add

1 cup fine noodles and the diced chicken. Cook an additional 10 minutes. SET A TIMER. Set aside to cool.

4. Package all remaining vegetables (except onions) in ziptop bags; include 4 cups cabbage for salads during the week. Zip the tops, leaving a 1-inch space for the vegetables to breathe. Refrigerate.

5. Assemble the sandwich fillings.

    Add diced onions to taste to the chopped eggs. Add enough mayonnaise to make a good spreading consistency and season with salt and pepper to taste. Place in a refrigerator container and refrigerate immediately.

    Drain the juice from about 2 tablespoons of sweet pickle relish. Add it to the chopped ham with enough mayonnaise to make a good spreading consistency. Place in a refrigerator container and refrigerate immediately.

6. Assemble two meat loaves.

    Put 3 pounds lean ground beef in a large bowl. Combine 4 eggs, 1 cup quick-cooking oatmeal, ¼ cup prepared mustard, ½ cup diced onion, 1 teaspoon salt, ¼ teaspoon pepper, 2 tablespoons Worcestershire sauce, and ½ cup milk in a blender container. Blend until smooth.

    Pour over the meat and add another ½ cup diced onion to the mixture. Mix thoroughly, using your hands if necessary.

    Divide into two 8½x4½x2½-inch meat-loaf pans, or 24 muffin cups, sprayed with vegetable oil (do not fill over the top of the tin). Cover one pan tightly and refrigerate it for Sunday. Overwrap the other and freeze it. (See the **Meat Loaf** recipe, p. 142, for a note on baking before freezing.)

7. Prepare the meats for the stir-fry recipes.

    Remove the partially frozen chicken breasts from the freezer and bone them. Remove the skin by pulling it off with your hands. Cut the whole breasts in half with a small sharp knife. Make a small cut between the flesh and the rib bones or the breast bone (it doesn't matter which side you start on). Now slip your thumb between the meat and the bones; you will be able to feel what you are doing, and the meat will come off easily. Use your knife only where necessary. Once you've done this a few times, you will be able to do it quickly. (Boneless chicken breasts prepared at home are one-third of the price of meat-market-prepared chickens.) Wrap breast pieces individually or in packages large enough for your family; freeze. They will be used for **Stir-Fried Chicken with Vegetables** on Tuesday.

    Remove the round steak from the freezer

and slice it in thin strips. Divide the strips into two food-safe freezer bags; freeze. One bag will be used for *Stir-Fried Beef and Snowpeas* on Friday; you will have another for a later meal.

8. Assemble the quiche base for two quiches.
   Measure 8 eggs, ¼ cup grated Parmesan cheese, ¼ cup water, 8 ounces chopped Swiss cheese, 2 dashes cayenne, 2 teaspoons onion powder, and ½ teaspoon salt (optional) into a blender container. Blend until smooth. In a small saucepan, sauté ½ cup diced onion in ¼ cup butter or margarine. Divide the sautéed onion into two freezer containers. Add half of the blender contents to each. Refrigerate one for Monday night and freeze the other for a later meal. Rinse the blender container.

Step 9
Finishing Food Preparation

Quick-and-Easy Pasta Sauce for four meals:

Spray a large, heavy, 8-quart saucepan with vegetable oil. Sauté 4 pounds ground beef with 2 cups chopped onions. When the beef loses its pink color, add 24 ounces tomato paste, 6 cups water, 2 tablespoons dried basil, 1 teaspoon garlic powder, ½ teaspoon crushed red pepper, and salt and pepper to taste. Bring the mixture to a boil, reduce the heat, and simmer uncovered for 15–20 minutes. Stir often. (Cover the pan with a spatter screen to prevent spattering all over your stove.) Set aside to cool.

Fried Chicken for four meals:

Put 4 eggs and 1 cup milk into a blender container and blend until smooth. Pour into a shallow pie plate. Measure 1 cup *Fried Chicken Coating Mix* (p. 64) into a plastic bag or medium-size bowl (add more as needed). Heat vegetable oil to 385° F in a heavy saucepan or electric skillet. Oil should be 1½ inches deep for deep fat frying.

Dip chicken legs, thighs, and breasts (from the refrigerator) in the egg mixture and shake off the excess. Coat with the seasoned coating mix and shake off the excess. (You can double-coat the chicken if you like a thick, crispy coating.) Fry the chicken pieces in hot oil, turning once, until golden brown on both sides. Drain on absorbent towels.

While the chicken is frying, use the extra minutes between pot-watching to remove the small pieces of meat from the backs, necks, and wings. Store this meat in freezer containers. Label and freeze.

Place the fried chicken pieces on large cookie sheets, freeze until frozen solid and then package loosely in food-safe freezer bags to be used as needed. To reheat, see recipe on p. 124.

Step 10
Package All Food

Label and date all containers and list the contents in your record of foods on hand.

☐ Put the cooled soups in refrigerator or freezer containers.

☐ Put any remaining diced onions in refrigerator containers or tray-freeze and package loosely in food-safe plastic bags.

☐ Take out enough hard rolls for Sunday; then overwrap and freeze the remainder in meal-size portions.

☐ Divide the French bread in half. Set aside half for tonight's (Saturday's) supper. Overwrap and freeze the other half for Wednesday.

☐ Refrigerate 4 cups of the cooked brown rice in a covered container for Tuesday and Friday. Freeze the remainder in meal-size portions.

☐ Divide the **Quick-and-Easy Pasta Sauce** into four 1-quart containers. Refrigerate one for Wednesday. Freeze the remainder for later meals (lasagna, pizza, stuffed manicotti, etc.).

☐ If you want homemade salad dressings, prepare and refrigerate.

Remember to label and date everything. List all foods stored in either the refrigerator or the freezer in a small notebook with the date they were stored.

Step 11
Clean Up and Relax!

☐ Put away all unused food products.

☐ Put away all unused cooking equipment.

☐ Wash all the dishes and clean up the cooking area.

☐ Before going to bed, package all tray-frozen foods.

☐ Take a well deserved rest!

My week's chain cooking might seem somewhat complicated: menu planning, grocery shopping, several hours of work on one day in the kitchen; but keep in mind that you will be free of all planning and most cooking chores for the entire week to come. You will even have extras on hand for many more meals in future weeks.

CHAPTER 4
USING THE WEEKLY MENU PLAN

Unless you can make proper use of the foods you prepared in advance, you lose all of the advantages of Chain Cooking. In the following pages we will take the menus from Chapter 3 and your well-stocked refrigerator and freezer and show you how to have dinner on the table with almost no effort. Remember that these foods have already been prepared by Chain Cooking, and you can relax while they are heating now.

Having a meal almost completely prepared in advance is like having a maid in the house. Desserts during the week can be kept very simple, consisting mostly of ice cream, fruit, or a simple-to-prepare dessert that can be made on a weekend or day off. (In the recipe section there are several delicious dessert recipes that can be prepared in a matter of minutes.) Menus in this chapter are planned for a family of four.

Saturday

Scalloped Potatoes
Baked Ham with Pineapple
Fresh vegetable salad
French bread with butter
Beverage
Ice Cream

☐ ☐ ☐

☐ **1½ hours before dinner:** Place the scalloped potatoes, covered, in a cold oven, and turn the oven to 375° F.

☐ **1 hour before dinner:** Prepare *Baked Ham with Pineapple,* p. 145. When you put the ham in the oven, uncover the potatoes.

☐ **10 minutes before dinner:** Place half a loaf of French bread in a brown paper bag, sprinkle the bag with cold water until it is lightly wet all over, close the top securely, and put the bag in the oven with the potatoes and the ham. The bread will be hot and crispy by serving time.

☐ Make a salad from the vegetables you prepared earlier during Chain Cooking.

☐ Remove the potatoes, ham, and bread from the oven and serve the dinner.

Sunday
Meat Loaf
Mashed Potatoes
Cabbage, Carrot, and Raisin Salad
Hard rolls with butter
Beverage
Strawberry Pie

□ □ □

□ **Early in the day,** at least 2 hours before dinner: make *Strawberry Pie,* p. 165. Refrigerate the pie, covered with plastic wrap, until serving time.

□ **1½ hours before dinner:** Place the meat loaf in a cold oven and set the temperature at 375° F.

□ **40 minutes before dinner:** Unwrap the refrigerated peeled potatoes, cut them in halves, and place them in a pan of hot tap water with 1 teaspoon salt. Cover, bring to a boil, cook until tender, and drain.

□ **15 minutes before dinner:** Prepare the *Cabbage, Carrot, and Raisin Salad,* p. 149.

□ Place the hard rolls in a brown paper bag, close the bag securely, and sprinkle the bag lightly with water until it is wet all over. Put the bag in the oven with the meat loaf. Set a timer for 5 minutes.

□ Mash the potatoes (see p. 29).

□ Remove the rolls and the meat loaf from the oven.

□ Serve the dinner.

Monday
Broccoli Quiche
Fresh vegetable salad
Hard rolls with butter
Beverage
Leftover Strawberry Pie

□ □ □

□ **30 minutes before dinner:** Preheat the oven to 350° F and assemble the Broccoli Quiche. Steam-cook 1½ cups frozen broccoli for 5 minutes; drain well. Spray a 9-inch Pyrex pie plate with vegetable oil. Put drained broccoli in the pie plate. Shake the refrigerated quiche mixture well and pour it over the broccoli. Bake in the preheated oven for 20 minutes or until a knife inserted halfway between the center and the outer edge comes out clean. Set a timer.

□ **10 minutes before dinner:** Prepare the rolls (see Sunday's menu, this page).

□ Make a salad from the vegetables you prepared during Chain Cooking.

□ Remove the quiche and the rolls from the oven.

□ Serve the dinner.

☐ **After dinner on Monday:** Prepare the *24-Hour Salad* for Tuesday's dinner, see p. 147. Refrigerate, cover tightly with plastic.

☐ Move the frozen chicken from the freezer to the refrigerator to defrost overnight.

Tuesday

Stir-Fried Chicken with Vegetables
Brown rice
24-Hour Salad
Bread and Butter
Beverage
Fresh fruit

☐ ☐ ☐

☐ **15 minutes before dinner:** Place 2 cups of cooked rice in a fine sieve or rice steamer over a pan of boiling water. Cover and steam 5–10 minutes or until heated through.

☐ Prepare the chicken with vegetables (p. 125).

☐ Serve the dinner.

Wednesday

Vermicelli with
Quick-and-Easy Pasta Sauce
Buttered corn
Cucumbers in sour cream
French bread with butter
(or garlic bread)
Beverage of choice
Ice cream

☐ ☐ ☐

☐ **20 minutes before dinner:** Preheat the oven to 400° F. Bring 4 quarts water with 1 tablespoon salt to a boil. Put the pasta sauce in a heavy 2-quart saucepan and heat over medium heat.

☐ **10 minutes before dinner:** Heat the French bread (see Saturday's menu. To make garlic bread (optional), slice the bread almost through to the bottom of the loaf; spread the slices with butter; sprinkle with garlic salt; and heat as you heated the bread in Saturday's menu.

☐ Cook the vermicelli in the boiling water according to the package directions.

☐ Heat the corn.

☐ Slice the cucumbers and put them in sour cream to cover.

☐ Drain and butter the corn. Remove the bread from the oven. Drain the vermicelli and pour the pasta sauce over it.

☐ Serve the dinner.

Thursday

Fried Chicken
Buttered egg noodles
Steamed carrots
Cabbage salad
Hot rolls with butter
Beverage
Peach Shortcake

☐ ☐ ☐

☐ **1 hour before dinner:** Preheat the oven to 425°F. Take the frozen whipped topping out of the freezer to defrost at room temperature for the shortcake.

☐ Put 8–12 pieces of frozen fried chicken on an ungreased cookie sheet; bake in the oven for 40–50 minutes (depending on the thickness of the pieces). Do not cover.

☐ **40 minutes before dinner:** Put peeled, refrigerated carrots in a steamer or fine sieve over boiling water; steam cook until tender.

☐ **15 minutes before dinner:** Mix 2 cups sliced or shredded cabbage, ¼ cup chopped green pepper, 1 tablespoon chopped onion, and enough mayonnaise to coat the vegetables lightly. Cover and return to the refrigerator until serving time.

☐ Cook the noodles according to the package directions.

☐ Prepare the rolls (see Sunday's menu).

☐ Mix the biscuits according to the recipe for *Rich Peach Shortcake*, p. 169.

☐ Remove the chicken and the rolls from the oven. Increase the oven temperature to 450° F and put the biscuits in the oven. Set a timer for 12–14 minutes. (The biscuits will bake while you are eating dinner and can be served warm.)

☐ Drain the noodles and toss them with 2 tablespoons butter for four servings.

☐ Serve the dinner.

☐ **After dinner on Thursday:** Move the thin-sliced beef for *Stir-Fried Beef and Snowpeas* from the freezer to the refrigerator to defrost overnight.

☐ Put the leftover frozen whipped topping in the refrigerator, so it will be thawed for Friday's dessert.

Friday

Stir-Fried Beef and Snowpeas
Brown rice
Fresh vegetable salad
Bread and butter
Beverage
Quick-and-Easy Chocolate Cake
with whipped topping

☐ ☐ ☐

☐ **45 minutes before dinner:** Prepare the *Quick-and-Easy Chocolate Cake* according to the recipe on p. 160.

☐ **15 minutes before dinner:** Put 2 cups of cooked rice in a fine sieve or rice steamer over boiling water; cover and steam until the rice is heated through, 5–10 minutes.

☐ Prepare the *Stir-Fried Beef* according to the recipe on p. 141.

☐ Make a salad from the vegetables you prepared during Chain Cooking.

☐ Remove the cake from the oven and put it on a wire rack to cool.

☐ Serve the dinner.

Leftovers for Future Meals:

If you got through your first week without any major problems, you should feel proud of your accomplishment. It will get easier every week. In addition, if you made everything in the work plan in Chapter 3, look at what you have left for future meals:

☐ 1 meat loaf or 12 miniatures

☐ 1 quiche base (just add your favorite vegetable)

☐ 3 quarts of *Quick-and-Easy Pasta Sauce*

☐ 3 meals of Fried Chicken

☐ 1 meal-size serving of brown rice

☐ 1 meal of thin-sliced beef for a stir-fry

Plan your next chain-cooking day to take advantage of these extra foods. Use the time to make a couple of extra casseroles (always in double recipes), stews, or possibly the *Big-Batch Meatballs* (p. 137) or *Pot Roast with Vegetable Gravy* (p. 138) to increase your meal choices in the coming weeks. Fill in with one or two of the simple fish dishes in the recipe section or a couple of the very easy and very good slow-cooker recipes that take just minutes to prepare early in the day, and are completely ready when you get home. You can even serve baked potatoes that were cooked all day, but taste just baked, right down to the crispy outside (see p. 103).

RECIPES

Read Well

Read all directions carefully before starting any recipe in this book since many recipes will presume that you have done your homework on the weekend and that some of the ingredients called for, such as a basic mix, will already be prepared.

For the purposes of this book, "low" means approximately 200° F (never less) and "high" means 275-300°F. Baking temperatures and times (except where noted) given are for Pyrex baking dishes because they brown food well and use lower oven temperatures. When using metal baking dishes, increase the oven temperature by 25 degrees.

All recipes in this book calling for flour have been tested with all-purpose unbleached flour. The results may differ with other types of flour.

Processed Foods

Occasionally there appears on the supermarket shelves a processed food product that is in fact an excellent food, even though it looks undesirable to those who prefer all-natural foods. It is important, therefore, to read the labels and ask oneself if the alternatives one prefers are sometimes even more harmful. I use two processed food products in this book; I'll explain why, and then I'll leave the choices up to you.

The first product is processed cheese (I recommend Velveeta®). People who are concerned about cardiovascular disease should use this instead of natural cheese, since it is lower in calories, fat, and cholesterol.

A second virtue of processed cheese is that it is emulsified in the same manner as homogenized milk to keep the fats and solids from separating. This is of significant value in recipes where the cheese will be cooked as a sauce, especially in slow-cookers. All natural cheeses separate, leaving the protein content of the cheese hard and granular, and sauces made with natural cheese thus tend to curdle easily. Processed cheese lends a creamy texture to many foods, and adds a rich, buttery, cheesy taste. When using it I can reduce fats and calories from butter and cream without sacrificing taste or texture even the slightest.

The other commercial product I recommend is frozen whipped topping. As well as being lower in fat, calories, and cholesterol than sweetened whipped cream, this product has a much longer shelf life. Real whipped cream is safe to eat for only two to three days, while frozen whipped toppings keep for weeks. The preservatives in the latter have all been cleared for safety, according to the Center for Science in the Public Interest.

CHAPTER 1
HOMEMADE MIXES

Make Your Own Mixes

Mixes are a great time-saver. They allow you to have homemade baked goods in a fraction of the time it takes to prepare them from scratch. Most people have a favorite muffin or cookie recipe that they would love to have as a mix if only they realized how easy it is. This recipe is a step-by-step method of creating mixes from your own recipes. These mixes must be made ahead of time.

Frequently, large jars for storing your homemade mixes can be obtained free of charge from delicatessens and restaurants. Plastic bags can also be used to store mixes. They are easy to measure from, and just shaking the bag will fluff up your mix. (Dry mixes should always be fluffed up with a fork or shaken lightly before measuring in order to get an accurate measure.) If you pre-measure homemade mixes into small ziptop plastic bags, you won't even have to stop to measure the mix when making your favorite recipe. Write out the directions for each mix and tape them to the container so you won't have to look for the recipe when you are in a hurry.

Mixes made with lard, real butter, or margarine must be refrigerated. Mixes made with vegetable shortening will stay fresh on the shelf for at least 2 months, and if your kitchen is cool they can be kept at room temperature much longer. For longer storage, refrigerate or freeze them.

1. Decide how many multiples of the recipe you want.
2. Write the multiples of all the dry ingredients right on the recipe, for example, 3 cups flour instead of one if you are tripling the recipe.
3. For each ¼ cup of liquid shortening, substitute **5 tablespoons** of solid vegetable shortening.
4. Place up to 3 cups of the dry ingredients and 1 cup of the solid shortening in a food processor bowl fitted with a steel chopping blade. Process until the shortening is com-

pletely incorporated (a few seconds). Empty the processor contents into a large mixing bowl. Continue processing batches of dry ingredients and shortening until all the ingredients are blended. If you don't have a food processor, use an electric mixer on high speed to cut in the ingredients until the mix is fine and crumbly.

5. Mix all the batches in the large mixing bowl, using a wire whisk. It is very important that all the ingredients are well distributed in the mix.

6. Measure the total amount of the mix.

7. Divide the number of cups of mix by the number of multiples you made; for example, if you have 12 cups mix and have tripled the recipe, divide 12 by 3. This tells you how much mix you will need to make a single recipe, in this case, 4. Write down the number of cups of mix you need on your recipe.

8. Store the mix in a labeled, tightly covered container at room temperature, and write out baking directions and tape them to the container.

9. **To make the recipe:** Measure the required amount of mix into a small to medium-size bowl. Measure the liquid ingredients into a blender container and blend until smooth. Pour the liquid ingredients over the dry mix and combine as directed in the original recipe, e.g., just enough to moisten the dry ingredients for muffins, or beating thoroughly for cakes. Bake according to the recipe directions.

Homemade Bread Mix

Makes 20 cups or enough for 6 large or 7 medium loaves. Any solid shortening may be used in this recipe. If you use a salted shortening, however, reduce the salt to 1½ tablespoons. Mixes made with liquid shortening must be refrigerated. The bowl I use to make this mix holds 8–10 quarts, or 32–40 cups.

14 cups all-purpose unbleached flour
2 tablespoons salt
1 cup sugar
1 cup vegetable shortening
4 cups stone-ground whole wheat flour (substitute all-white or rye or graham flour, if desired)

1. Mix 3½ cups of the all-purpose flour, 1½ teaspoons salt, ¼ cup sugar, and ¼ cup shortening in a food-processor bowl fitted with a steel chopping blade. Process until the dough is the consistency of cornmeal. Empty the mix into a very large bowl.
2. Repeat three more times until all of the all-purpose flour is used up.
3. Add 4 cups of whole wheat (white, rye, or graham) flour to the contents of the bowl. Mix thoroughly with a wire whisk to incorporate all the ingredients evenly.
4. Store in a large, covered container at room temperature.

Chocolate Cake Mix

Makes 10 cups, enough for 4 single layer cakes.

6 cups all-purpose unbleached flour
4 cups sugar
2 teaspoons salt
4 teaspoons baking soda
1 cup unsweetened cocoa

1. Measure the first four ingredients into a very large bowl.
2. Sift the cocoa over the other ingredients.
3. Mix *thoroughly* with a wire whisk to incorporate all ingredients.
4. Store in a covered container at room temperature.

Fried Chicken Coating Mix

Makes about 5 cups. This recipe may also be used to coat fried fish.

- 4 cups all-purpose unbleached flour
- 4 teaspoons garlic powder
- 1 tablespoon oregano
- 2 tablespoons dried parsley
- 2 tablespoons dried basil
- 1½ teaspoons dried sweet marjoram
- 1½ teaspoons dried thyme
- 4 teaspoons salt
- 1 teaspoon pepper
- 1 tablespoon paprika
- 1 tablespoon sugar (optional, used for browning agent)

1. Place all the ingredients in a large bowl and mix well with a wire whisk. Be sure to incorporate all ingredients.
2. Store in a covered container at room temperature.

Crumbs for Toppings

This recipe is the perfect solution for bread, rolls, or crackers that have gone stale.

Stale bread or roll, or cracker crumbs
4 teaspoons butter or margarine for each cup of breadcrumbs, or each ½ cup of cracker crumbs

1. Break the bread, rolls, or crackers into a food processor container fitted with a steel chopping blade. Add the recommended amount of butter.
2. Process the bread until crumbed. Butter will coat the crumbs evenly.
3. Pour the crumbs onto a cookie sheet and tray freeze.
4. Package the crumbs in food-safe plastic bags to be used as needed to top casserole dishes.

Fruit Crisp Topping

Makes $5\frac{1}{3}$ cups, enough for about 4 fruit crisps.

1 cup butter or margarine
$1\frac{1}{3}$ cups brown sugar, packed
1½ cups all-purpose unbleached flour
1½ cups quick-cooking oatmeal
1 teaspoon nutmeg
3 teaspoons cinnamon
½ cup toasted wheat germ or bran buds

1. Measure all the ingredients into a food processor bowl fitted with a steel chopping blade. Process until the mixture resembles cornmeal.
2. Store the topping in a food-safe plastic bag or covered container in the refrigerator.

Graham Cracker Pie Crust Mix

Makes 7 cups, enough for 4 crusts. This quick-and-easy crust is an excellent choice for pudding pies and can even be used to make pie out of the molded desserts on pp. 173–174.

5 cups finely crushed graham crackers
1 cup sugar
1 teaspoon cinnamon
1 stick cold butter or margarine, cut into chunks

1. Measure 2½ cups graham cracker crumbs into a food processor bowl fitted with a steel chopping blade.
2. Add ½ cup sugar, ½ teaspoon cinnamon, and ½ stick butter to the bowl. Process until the dough is crumbly and no butter chunks are visible.
3. Repeat with the remaining crackers, sugar, cinnamon, and butter.
4. Combine the mixtures.
5. Store the mix in a food-safe plastic bag in the refrigerator. It will keep indefinitely.

To make pie crust: Preheat the oven to 375°F. Measure 1¾ cups of mix into a 9-inch pie plate sprayed with vegetable oil. Press the crust against the bottom of the pie plate with the palm of your hand and against the sides with the back of your hand to make the crust hold its shape in the pie plate. Bake in the preheated oven for 8 minutes if you are filling with a cold mixture, or for 5 minutes if you are filling with a mixture that must be baked.

Homemade Pie Crust Mix

Makes 8 cups, enough for 3 2-crust pies or 6 1-crust pies. I have not put any recipes that call for pie crust in this book since most busy people find it too time-consuming to make them. If you like pies with crusts, however, this recipe will save you time.

6 cups all-purpose unbleached flour
1 teaspoon salt
2 cups solid vegetable shortening

1. Measure 3 cups of the flour into a food processor bowl fitted with a steel chopping blade.
2. Add ½ teaspoon salt and 1 cup shortening and process until crumbly. Do not overprocess.
3. Repeat with the remaining flour, salt, and shortening.
4. Store in a covered container in a cool area.

To make pie crust: Measure 2⅔ cups pie crust mix into a medium-size bowl. Stir in 4–5 tablespoons ice water. Use just enough water to hold the dough together; it should not be wet. Let stand for 5 minutes. Divide the dough in half and roll it out to fit a pie plate. Proceed as the pie recipe directs. (To make a single-crust pie, use only 1⅓ cups of mix and about 3 tablespoons of ice water.)

Baking Powder Biscuit Mix

Makes 12 cups of mix (enough for 48 biscuits). Any solid shortening may be used in this recipe, including butter, margarine, or lard. When using salted butter or margarine, reduce the salt to 1 teaspoon.

8 cups all-purpose unbleached flour
1/3 cup baking powder
2 teaspoons salt
2 teaspoons cream of tartar
4 teaspoons sugar
2 cups vegetable shortening

1. Put 4 cups of the flour, the baking powder, salt, cream of tartar, sugar, and 1 cup of shortening in a food processor bowl fitted with a steel chopping blade. Process until the mix is the consistency of cornmeal. Pour into a large bowl.

2. Put the remaining 4 cups of flour and 1 cup of shortening in the processor bowl and proceed as above.

3. Mix the two batches *thoroughly,* using a wire whisk.

4. Refrigerate.

Cornbread Mix

Makes 15 cups or 4 large cornbreads or 6 smaller ones. This mix makes the best cornbread I have ever eaten.

9 cups all-purpose unbleached flour
3 cups cornmeal
4 teaspoons salt
4 tablespoons baking powder
3 cups sugar

1. Mix all the ingredients in a large bowl with a wire whisk. Be sure to incorporate all the ingredients evenly.

2. Store in a covered container at room temperature.

Bran Muffins

Makes approximately 5 dozen muffins. This mix is complete. Just fill your muffin tins and bake, and you can have hot muffins anytime. It will keep in the refrigerator for up to six weeks. You will need a storage container that holds 5 quarts, or 20 cups.

2 cups boiling water
2 cups all-bran cereal
5 cups all-purpose unbleached flour
5 teaspoons baking soda
2 teaspoons salt
1 cup sugar
½ cup honey
1 cup solid vegetable shortening
4 eggs
1 quart buttermilk
4 cups Grapenuts cereal

1. Pour the boiling water over the all-bran cereal and stir well. Set aside to cool.

2. Measure the flour, baking soda, salt, and sugar into a large mixing bowl. Stir well with a wire whisk to mix.

3. Measure the honey, vegetable shortening, eggs, and 2 cups of buttermilk into a blender container. Blend until smooth.

4. Pour the blender contents over the dry ingredients. Add the remaining 2 cups of buttermilk, the Grapenuts cereal and the all-bran mixture. Stir to mix, but do not overmix. All ingredients should be wet, but the dough should still be lumpy.

5. Store in a covered container in the refrigerator for up to six weeks.

To bake: Spray muffin tins with vegetable oil. Then fill the tins two-thirds full with muffin mix and bake in a preheated oven set at 400°F. for 20–25 minutes or until browned. Serve hot.

Instant Herbed Rice Mix

Makes 6 cups mix, enough to make 12 cups rice. Instant rice (rice that is added to boiling water and is ready in 5 minutes) does not contain the nutrients of brown or long-grain rice; however, in a pinch it is still better for you than frozen french fries or greasy potato chips. The additions to the rice, such as vegetables in fried rice, or raisins and milk in rice pudding, make up for lack of nutrients in the rice.

12 CUPS

- 6 cups instant rice
- 2 tablespoons dried celery flakes
- 3 tablespoons dried chives
- 2 tablespoons dried parsley
- ½ cup dehydrated instant onion

1. Mix all the ingredients well.
2. Store in a covered container at room temperature.

To make rice: Cook ⅓ cup rice with ⅓ cup water or broth, ⅛ teaspoon salt, and ½ teaspoon butter for each serving. (For a softer rice, add 1 more tablespoon of water per serving.) Bring the broth to a boil, stir in the rice and seasonings, remove from the heat, cover, and let stand for 5 minutes (8 minutes if you have added extra broth or water). Remove the cover, fluff the rice with a fork, and serve.

CHAPTER 2
BREAD AND ROLLS

You're dreaming of freshly baked, homemade bread, but the dream turns to a nostalgic sigh when the clanging of your alarm clock reminds you that working people don't have time to bake bread. Not true! With this bread mix, the new quick-rising yeasts, and my new techniques for making brown-and-serve breads and rolls, you can have hot homemade bread in just 30 minutes — rolls in less — anytime you want them.

This homemade bread is very easy to make, but be sure to follow directions exactly and use the recommended type of ingredients, especially the all-purpose unbleached flour and the quick-rising yeast. Breads made only with all-purpose unbleached flour rise faster and higher than those made with heavier, coarser flours.

Starting yeast bread in a cold oven makes it rise more evenly and eliminates air pockets.

Most cooks eliminate kneading completely when making bread with a food processor, and you can, too; however, I have found that the very brief kneading that I call for produces a higher, lighter loaf that rises faster.

Homemade Bread

1 LARGE LOAF.

3⅓ cups *Homemade Bread Mix*, p. 63, stirred well before measuring
1 package quick-rising dry yeast
¾–1 cup hot tap water (120–130° F)

You will need a bread pan that measures 9x5x3 for this recipe. If you want to make a smaller loaf (8½x4x2½), see the Variation at the end of this recipe.

1. Measure the well-stirred mix into a food processor bowl fitted with a steel chopping blade.
2. Add the dry yeast.
3. With the processor running, slowly pour in ¾ cup hot tap water. The dough should form a ball that leaves the sides of the bowl. If it does not, add more water, a little at a time. The dough should feel sticky and should try to stick to the sides of the bowl, but it should not actually stick. Let the ball of dough revolve around the bowl 45 times.
4. Turn the dough out onto a clean countertop. (If the dough sticks to the countertop, it's too wet; add more mix 1 tablespoon at a time.) Knead the dough 20 times.
5. Form the dough into a ball and place in a 9x5x3-inch bread pan sprayed with vegetable oil. Turn once to coat the dough with the vegetable oil. Cover with oiled wax paper and a light towel. Place in a warm spot, free from drafts, and let rise for 10 minutes.
6. Punch down the dough. Turn it out onto a clean countertop and knead it 10 times.
7. Shape the dough into a loaf and return it to the pan. Cover again using the same wax paper. Let the dough rise again until it is slightly more than double. It should come to just a little over the top of the bread pan.

8. Place the bread in a *cold oven* and set the oven temperature to 375°F. Bake for 30–35 minutes or until the top sounds hollow when tapped and is very brown.

9. Remove the bread from the oven and brush the top with melted butter if desired.

10. Remove from the pan and cool on a wire rack.

Variation:
To make a slightly smaller loaf, use 2 cups plus 3 tablespoons **Homemade Bread Mix,** 1 package quick-rising dry yeast, and ⅔–¾ cup hot tap water.

Baking Powder Biscuits

6–8 BISCUITS

1½ cups *Baking Powder Biscuit Mix,* p. 68, stirred well before measuring
⅓ cup cold milk

For a real treat, serve these hot biscuits with butter and honey and a cup of your favorite tea.

1. Preheat the oven to 450°F.
2. Combine the mix and the milk in a small bowl.
3. Stir well with a fork until a slightly stiff dough is formed.
4. With a tablespoon, mound biscuits onto a baking sheet that has been sprayed with vegetable oil.
5. Bake in the preheated oven for 12–14 minutes or until the biscuits are golden brown on top.

Variations:
For shortcake biscuits, add 1 tablespoon sugar to the dry mix before adding the milk.
To make biscuits for creamed chicken or turkey, add ¼ teaspoon poultry seasoning to the mix before adding the milk.

Brown-and-Serve Bread

1 LARGE LOAF

3⅓ cups *Homemade Bread Mix*, p. 63, stirred well before measuring
1 package quick-rising dry yeast
¾-1 cup hot tap water (120-130° F)

1. Make *Homemade Bread* according to the recipe directions on p. 72 through step #7.
2. Cover the bread lightly with foil.
3. Place it in a cold oven set at 350°F. Bake for 15 minutes. Remove the foil, reduce the heat to 250°F., and bake for an additional 10 minutes.
4. Remove the bread from the oven. Remove from the pan and cool on a wire rack.
5. Wrap with food-safe freezer wrap and freeze.

To Bake: Preheat oven to 400°F. Place defrosted bread in a metal bread tin. Bake 15-20 minutes until nicely browned and the bread sounds hollow when tapped on top. Remove from the oven. Remove from the tin and brush the top with butter or margarine. Cool on a wire rack. The outside will be crispy and the inside will be soft and delicious. Breads baked this way are slightly heavier than other breads.

Variation:
This bread can be defrosted at room temperature and then baked. Cover the bread lightly with foil and place it in a cold oven set at 375°F. Bake for 15 minutes. Uncover and continue baking for 8-10 minutes longer.

Seasoned Croutons

You can make the equivalent of two large boxes of croutons for less than half the price of a single box. Vary the seasonings to suit yourself. The loaf of bread that this recipe produces is too heavy to be very good as bread. It's better as croutons.

7 CUPS

- 3 cups *Homemade Bread Mix,* p. 63, stirred well before measuring
- 1 package quick-rising yeast
- ½ cup grated Parmesan cheese (dry variety)
- 1½ tablespoons dried parsley
- 2 teaspoons dried chives
- 1 tablespoon garlic powder
- 2 teaspoons salt (optional)
- 1 cup hot tap water (120-130°F), more or less, as needed to make a soft dough

1. Measure all the ingredients except the water into a food-processor bowl fitted with a steel chopping blade.
2. Make the bread according to the directions for *Homemade Bread,* p. 72.
3. When the bread is one or two days old, slice it and cut the slices into small cubes. Place the cubes in single layers on cookie sheets. Put the cookie sheets in a 200°F. oven and bake for 15 minutes. Set a timer so you won't forget.
4. Turn off the heat and leave the cubes in the oven until they are very dry. Stir occasionally. (To hurry the process, you can turn on the oven for a few minutes every hour or so.)
5. Place the completely cooled croutons in a tightly covered container and store at room temperature.

Homemade Bread Stuffing

When you find out how easy it is to make this delicious stuffing, you'll never want to buy prepared stuffing again. The savings alone are worth the effort. You can make the equivalent of four 8-ounce packages for less than the price of one.

1½ POUNDS STUFFING CRUMBS

- 3 cups *Homemade Bread Mix,* p. 63, stirred well before measuring
- 1 package quick-rising dry yeast
- 1 tablespoon poultry seasoning
- 1½ teaspoons ground sage
- ¾ teaspoon pepper
- 1 tablespoon onion powder
- 1 tablespoon plus 1 teaspoon chicken bouillon powder
- 2 tablespoons dried parsley
- 1 tablespoon dried celery flakes
- ¾–1 cup hot tap water (120–130°F)

1. Measure all the dry ingredients into a food processor fitted with a steel blade.
2. Make the bread according to the directions for *Homemade Bread,* p. 72.
3. Let the cooled bread stand at room temperature, uncovered, for 24 hours.
4. Slice the bread into thick slices and tear them into the food processor fitted with a steel blade. Process the bread into coarse crumbs and pour the crumbs onto large cookie sheets. Put the cookie sheets of crumbs into a 200°F. oven. Bake for 10 minutes. Set a timer so you won't forget.
5. Turn off the heat, leaving the crumbs in the oven until they are very dry; stir occasionally. (To hurry the process you can turn on the oven for a few minutes every hour or so.)
6. Place the completely cooled crumbs in a tightly covered container and store at room temperature or freeze.

Pumpkin Bread

2 LARGE LOAVES

3 cups *Baking Powder Biscuit Mix*, p. 68, stirred well before measuring
3 teaspoons cinnamon
1 teaspoon cloves
1 teaspoon salt
1 cup chopped walnuts
1 cup raisins
⅓ cup vegetable oil
¾ cup brown sugar
4 eggs
2 teaspoons vanilla extract
2 cups canned pumpkin

1. Preheat the oven to 350°F.
2. Measure the biscuit mix, cinnamon, cloves, and salt into a large mixing bowl. Stir well to mix. Remove 2 tablespoons and combine with the walnuts and raisins. This will suspend them in the batter and prevent them from sinking to the bottom.
3. Measure the oil, brown sugar, eggs, vanilla, and pumpkin into a blender container and blend until smooth.
4. Pour the blender contents over the dry ingredients. Mix thoroughly, but do not beat. Stir in the walnut-raisin mixture.
5. Divide the batter into two 9x5x3-inch loaf tins sprayed with vegetable oil.
6. Bake in the preheated oven for 45–55 minutes, or until a toothpick inserted in the center of each loaf comes out clean.
7. Cool in the loaf pans for 5 minutes; then remove from the pans and finish cooling on wire racks.

Cloverleaf Rolls

1 DOZEN

3 cups *Homemade Bread Mix,* p. 63, stirred well before measuring
1 package quick-rising dry yeast
2 tablespoons sugar
1 egg
½ cup hot tap water (120-130°F), more or less, as needed to make a soft dough

For a soft crust, brush the tops of the warm rolls with melted butter.

1. Measure the well-stirred mix into a food processor bowl fitted with a steel chopping blade.
2. Add the dry yeast, sugar, and unbeaten egg.
3. With the food processor running, slowly pour in the hot tap water. The dough should form a ball that leaves the sides of the bowl; if it does not, add more water, a little at a time. The dough should feel sticky and should try to stick to the sides of the bowl, but it should not actually stick. Let the ball of dough revolve around the bowl 45 times.
4. Turn the dough out onto a clean countertop. (If the dough sticks to the countertop, it's too wet; add more mix 1 tablespoon at a time.) Knead the dough 20 times.
5. Form the dough into a ball and place it in a bowl sprayed with vegetable oil. Turn once to coat the dough with the oil. Cover the bowl with oiled wax paper and a light towel. Place in a warm spot, free from drafts. Let the dough rise for 10 minutes.
6. Punch down the dough. Knead it 10 times.
7. Shape the dough into 1-inch round balls and place three balls in each of twelve muffin cups that have been sprayed with vegetable oil.
8. Let the dough rise until it is slightly more than double.
9. Put the baking tin in a *cold* oven and set the oven tempera-

ture to 350°F. Bake for 20–25 minutes or until the top is golden brown.

10. Remove the rolls from the tin and cool on a wire rack.

Cornbread

12 SERVINGS

3¾ cups *Cornbread Mix* (p. 68). stirred well before measuring
2 eggs
1½ cups milk
1 tablespoon butter, melted

1. Preheat the oven to 400°F.
2. Measure the well-stirred mix into a medium-size bowl.
3. Put the remaining ingredients in a blender container and blend until smooth.
4. Pour the blender contents over the mix and stir only until the ingredients are moistened. Do not overmix.
5. Pour into a 9x13-inch Pyrex baking dish sprayed with vegetable oil.
6. Bake in the preheated oven for about 30 minutes, or until a toothpick inserted into the center comes out clean. Serve warm.

Variations:
    For Mexican cornbread, add 1 small minced jalapeno pepper to the mixture.
    For double-corn cornbread, add ¾ cup cooked, well-drained, whole-kernel corn to the mixture.

Croissants

In all my years of cooking, I have never found an easier or more delicious croissant than these. It's an ideal recipe for busy people, because it makes so many, and they can be frozen. This refrigerator dough keeps for up to four days so you can have fresh rolls daily even without a freezer.

The dough for the croissants must be refrigerated for at least 4 hours before baking. To make these rolls without a food processor, cut the batter into the flour with an electric mixer or a pastry blender.

They are best served warm.

32 CROISSANTS

- 1 cup warm tap water (115°F.)
- 1 package regular dry yeast
- 2/3 cup light whipping cream
- 1/3 cup sugar
- 2 eggs
- 1½ teaspoons salt
- 5¼ cups all-purpose unbleached flour
- ¼ cup butter or margarine, melted and cooled
- 1 cup cold butter or margarine, cut into ½-inch slices
- 1 tablespoon cold water

1. Warm a 1-quart bowl by rinsing it with hot water. Then combine the warm water and the yeast in the bowl. Stir to dissolve the yeast.

2. Add the cream, sugar, 1 egg, the salt, and 1 cup of the flour.

3. Beat the mixture with a wire whisk to make a smooth batter. Blend in the melted butter. Set the batter aside.

4. Measure 3 cups of the remaining flour into a food processor bowl fitted with a steel chopping blade. Slice the cold butter into the flour. Process using the pulse button, off and on, until the butter is in pieces no larger than a small dried bean. Transfer the mixture to a large mixing bowl and stir in the remaining 1¼ cups of flour.

5. Pour the yeast mixture over the flour mixture. Stir with a wooden spoon just until all the flour is moistened. Cover tightly and refrigerate for at least 4 hours, or up to 4 days.

6. Turn the chilled dough onto a lightly floured surface. Knead several times to soften the dough. Divide the dough into four equal parts. If you are going to bake all the rolls at once, keep the quarters of dough that you are not working with in the refrigerator until needed. If you aren't going to bake them all at once, the dough can be kept in the refrigerator for up to 4 days.

7. Roll each quarter into a circle about 16 inches in diameter. Cut into eight equal pie-shaped wedges. Roll up each wedge, starting at the wide end and rolling to the point.

8. Place the croissants about 1½ inches apart on ungreased cookie sheets. Curve the ends of each roll to form a crescent. Cover the croissants loosely with plastic wrap and let them stand in a very warm place (85°F.) until they have slightly more than doubled.

9. Mix the 1 remaining egg with the cold water and brush on the rolls just before baking.

10. Place the rolls in a *cold* oven and set the oven temperature to 325°F. Bake the rolls until golden, 20–25 minutes.

11. Remove from the cookie sheets and cool on wire racks.

Variation:

Brown-and-Serve Croissants: Prepare the croissants as directed right up to the baking. Place them in a *cold* oven and set the temperature to 200°F. Bake for 20 minutes. Remove from the oven and cool on the baking sheets. Freeze on the baking sheets. When they are frozen, transfer the rolls to food-safe plastic freezer bags. To bake, place the frozen rolls on a baking sheet, place in a cold oven, and set the oven temperature to 350°F. Bake for 12–14 minutes or until golden brown.

Quick-and-Easy French Bread

This bread can be made from start to finish in 60 minutes.

1 LARGE LOAF

2½ cups all-purpose un-
   bleached flour
2 teaspoons vegetable oil
2 teaspoons sugar
1½ teaspoons salt
1 package quick-rising yeast
   (approximately 1 tablespoon)
¾–1 cup hot tap water (120–
   130°F)
cornmeal
1 egg
1 tablespoon water

1. Measure the flour, oil, sugar, salt, and yeast into a food processor bowl fitted with a steel chopping blade.

2. With the processor going, slowly pour in ¾ cup water until the dough forms a ball and leaves the sides of the bowl. Add more water, if necessary, a little at a time. The dough should feel sticky and should try to stick to the sides of the bowl, but it should not actually stick. Let the ball of dough revolve around the bowl 35 times.

3. Knead the dough on a clean countertop 20 times.

4. Place the dough in a bowl sprayed with vegetable oil. Turn the dough over once to coat it with oil. Cover the bowl with oiled wax paper and a light towel. Let the dough rise in a very warm place, free of drafts. Every 5 minutes, punch down the dough and knead it 5 times. Set a timer to save confusion. Do this 5 times.

5. After punching down the dough the last time, roll it out onto a lightly floured board to a 9x12 rectangle. Roll up the dough jelly-roll fashion. Then pinch the ends and the seam to seal the loaf.

6. Spray a cookie sheet lightly with vegetable oil and sprinkle it with cornmeal.

7. Place the rolled bread on the cookie sheet. Cut four diagonal slashes on the top of the bread.

8. Cover again with the wax paper and a light towel and let rise for 10 minutes.//
9. Mix the egg with the water until the mixture is foamy. Brush over the top of the bread.
10. Put the bread into a *cold* oven and set the oven temperature to 350°F. Bake for 25–30 minutes or until the bread is golden brown.
11. Cool on a wire rack.

Sticky Buns

1 DOZEN

- 2 cups plus 3 tablespoons *Homemade Bread Mix,* p. 63, stirred well before measuring
- 1 package quick-rising dry yeast
- ⅔–¾ cup hot tap water
- 3 tablespoons sugar
- ⅔ teaspoon cinnamon
- ⅓ cup light brown sugar, packed
- ⅓ cup dark corn syrup
- 2 tablespoons butter or margarine
- ½ cup walnut or pecan halves
- ¼ cup raisins

1. Make the bread dough according to the recipe directions for **Homemade Bread,** p. 72.
2. Roll out the dough to a 10x14-inch rectangle.
3. Combine the sugar and cinnamon and sprinkle the dough with the cinnamon-sugar and the raisins.
4. Roll up the dough jellyroll fashion and pinch seam to seal.
5. With a long, sharp knife, cut the dough into 1-inch slices. Let them rest while you prepare the syrup.
6. Mix the brown sugar, corn syrup, and butter in a small saucepan. Bring to a boil, stirring constantly. Pour the syrup into a 9-inch round baking dish sprayed with vegetable oil.
7. Arrange the nuts evenly in the syrup.
8. Arrange the roll slices in the syrup, leaving ½ inch between each slice.
9. Cover with oiled wax paper and a light towel. Let the rolls rise in a warm place, free from drafts until they are double in bulk (about 30 minutes).
10. Place in a *cold* oven. Set the oven temperature to 375°F. Bake for 17–22 minutes until golden brown.
11. Immediately invert the buns onto a large serving plate and leave the baking dish in place on top of them to let all the syrup drizzle down. Serve warm.

CHAPTER 3
SOUPS

Rich Chicken Broth

Save carcasses from roasted chicken, or necks, backs, wings, and gizzards from frying chickens until you have a potful to make this broth Or cook a large fowl in water, and you will have a rich broth plus nice chunks of chicken for salads, soups, or casseroles.

3 QUARTS

1 large carrot, scraped and coarsely chopped
1 large onion, coarsely chopped
1 large celery stalk, or 1 cup celery leaves
2 cups water
1 tablespoon salt
½ teaspoon pepper
¼ cup fresh parsley
5 pounds chicken carcasses, parts, or whole fowl
1 tablespoon cider vinegar
water

1. Put the vegetables in a blender with 2 cups water. Blend until the vegetables are puréed. (This will give the broth a better flavor and richer color.)

2. Pour the vegetables into a slow-cooker or large soup kettle. Add the seasonings, parsley, and chicken. Add water to cover and cover the pan.

3. Cook on low (200°F) for 24 hours in a slow-cooker, 4–6 hours on the stove, or 12–24 hours on a woodstove.

4. Strain the broth and chill it overnight. Skim off most of the fat. Package the broth in freezer containers and freeze. Or, if you are short of freezer space, reduce the broth to one-fourth its volume and store it in the refrigerator indefinitely (see note p. 33). To reconstitute the condensed broth, combine 1 part broth with 3 parts water. Use for soup, gravies, and sauces.

Homemade Beef Stock

Economical beef stock can be made from beef trimmings, leftover pieces of beef, bones from steaks and roasts, and extra bits of leftover ground beef. Put all of these away in a freezer bag until you have about 5 pounds or enough to fill your slow-cooker. Be sure to include some fat; fat lends a sweet flavor to the broth. The broth can be chilled and the fat removed after cooking, and the flavor will remain. If your slow-cooker will not hold 5 pounds (if it is less than a 5-quart slow-cooker), weigh what it will hold and reduce the ingredients in this recipe accordingly. Broths produced from cooking vegetables make a welcome flavor addition to this recipe. Don't use broths from strong-flavored vegetables such as broccoli and cabbage.

4 QUARTS

- 2 large carrots, scraped and coarsely chopped
- 1 large onion, chopped
- 1 cup chopped celery leaves (include some celery if desired)
- 1 small white turnip, chopped (optional)
- 4-5 pounds beef trimmings and/or bones
- 1 tablespoon salt
- ¼ teaspoon pepper
- 1 tablespoon cider vinegar
- water and/or vegetable juices to fill the pot

1. Combine all the ingredients in a slow-cooker or large soup kettle.

2. Cook in a slow-cooker set on low (200°F.) for 24 hours (the broth will be very rich) or on top of the stove for 3–4 hours. If you are lucky enough to have a woodstove, simmer on top of the woodstove for 12–24 hours.

3. Strain the broth. Chill overnight or for several hours. Remove most of the congealed fat. Pack in freezer containers and freeze. Or reduce the broth to one-fourth its volume and store it in refrigerator containers (see note p. 33).

Instant Rice Soup

4–6 SERVINGS

4 cups *Rich Chicken Broth*, p. 85, or canned broth
¾ cup *Instant Herbed Rice Mix*, p. 70
2 tablespoons rendered chicken fat, butter, or margarine
½ teaspoon salt (omit with canned broth)

This soup can be made with beef or vegetable broth instead of chicken broth.

1. Bring the broth to a boil in a 1½–2-quart covered saucepan.
2. Stir in the rice mix, rendered chicken fat, and salt. Cover, remove from the heat, and let stand for 10 minutes.

Instant Iced Avocado Soup

4–6 SERVINGS

1¼ cups mashed avocado (2–3 large avocados)
3 cups *Rich Chicken Broth*, p. 85, or canned broth
1 cup light cream
½ teaspoon salt (or more to taste)
dash white pepper
dash cayenne
1½ teaspoons onion powder
minced fresh chives

The avocados in this recipe should be very ripe. For an elegant first course, serve this soup in iced champagne glasses.

1. Measure all the ingredients, except the chives, into a blender container. Purée until smooth. (If you have a small blender, you may have to do two batches.)
2. Chill for a half-hour before serving, to blend the flavors.
3. Serve topped with the fresh chives.

Instant Jellied Consommé

Freeze chicken or beef broth in ice cube trays and then empty the trays loosely into food-safe plastic bags. Keep these cubes on hand all the time to impress your guests with this quick and easy consommé made 10 minutes before serving.

4–6 SERVINGS

2 packages unflavored gelatin
2 cups canned beef or chicken broth
1 teaspoon tomato paste (omit with chicken broth)
2 cups frozen beef or chicken broth cubes
2 tablespoons marsala (for beef) or sherry (for chicken) (optional)
salt to taste
dash cayenne
small sprigs fresh parsley

1. Soften the gelatin in *1 cup* of cold broth in a small saucepan for 1 minute. Heat to dissolve the gelatin. Then stir in the tomato paste.

2. Measure 2 cups of broth cubes. Add water or additional broth to bring the liquid up to the 2-cup line.

3. Pour the heated mixture into a medium-size, heat-proof bowl. Add the remaining cup of broth and the iced broth. Stir in the wine and the seasonings (except the parsley).

4. Keep stirring to dissolve the ice cubes. When the mixture becomes thick, refrigerate it for 5 minutes. Then stir again and remove any remaining ice. Cover and keep chilled until serving time.

5. To serve, rake through the consommé with a wide tined fork to create a light, airy effect. Spoon into chilled serving dishes. Garnish with sprigs of parsley.

Instant Squash Bisque

4 SERVINGS

½ cup diced onion
½ cup diced celery
2 tablespoons butter or margarine
1½ cups frozen winter squash
2 cups *Rich Chicken Broth*, p. 85, or canned broth
pinch ground cloves
salt and pepper to taste
½ cup canned, drained mushrooms, chopped
½ cup light cream

1. Sauté the onion and celery in butter or margarine.
2. Add the squash, chicken broth, and seasonings. Bring to a boil and reduce the heat. Cook covered for 10 minutes.
3. Add the mushrooms and cream. Preheat just until piping hot. Do not boil.
4. Adjust the seasonings and serve.

Instant Egg Drop Soup

4 SERVINGS

½ cup sliced scallions
1 tablespoon minced fresh parsley
1 tablespoon butter or margarine
4 cups *Rich Chicken Broth*, p. 85, or canned broth
2 eggs, slightly beaten with a fork
salt and pepper to taste

1. Sauté the scallions and parsley in butter.
2. Add the chicken broth and bring to a boil.
3. With the broth boiling gently, slowly stir in the lightly beaten egg with a fork.
4. Shut off the heat, cover and let stand for 5 minutes to set the eggs.
5. Add salt and pepper. Serve.

Tomato Cheese Soup

Combine a ham-and-cheese sandwich with this super-quick, absolutely delicious soup and curl up for a Sunday afternoon football game, the first snowfall, an après ski party, or decorating the Christmas tree. Add a favorite beverage and everyone will be happy.

4 SERVINGS

4 cups canned tomatoes with their juice
1 medium-size onion, cut in small chunks
6 ounces Velveeta® cheese
salt and pepper to taste

1. Cook the tomatoes and onion in a medium-size covered saucepan until the onion is tender, about 10 minutes.
2. Pour the tomato mixture into a blender container with the cheese and the salt and pepper. Purée until very smooth.
3. Return to the saucepan and reheat until just piping hot. Do not boil. Serve.

Corn Chowder

6 SERVINGS

1 large onion, diced
2 tablespoons bacon fat, butter, or margarine
2 large potatoes, diced small
salt and pepper to taste
2 cups canned whole-kernel corn
1 cup canned cream-style corn
3-4 cups milk or half-and-half

1. Sauté the onion in the bacon fat in a medium-size, covered saucepan until it is limp but not brown.
2. Add the diced potatoes and enough water to cover. Season with salt and pepper.
3. Cover the pan and simmer the potatoes until they are tender.
4. Add the remaining ingredients and heat to simmering.
5. Adjust the seasonings.
6. Cover and let stand for 15 minutes to blend the flavors before serving.

Super-Quick Cauliflower Cheddar Soup

4–6 SERVINGS

16 ounces frozen cauliflower
3 cups *Rich Chicken Broth*, **p. 85, or canned broth**
1 tablespoon butter or margarine
4 ounces extra-sharp cheddar cheese
2 tablespoons grated Parmesan cheese
2 ounces leftover boiled or mashed potato
salt and pepper to taste
minced parsley

1. Cook the cauliflower in the chicken broth in a covered pan until tender, about 10 minutes.
2. Measure the remaining ingredients (except the parsley) into a blender container.
3. Remove several pieces of cauliflower from the pan with a slotted spoon and set them aside.
4. Add the remaining cauliflower and broth to the blender container. Purée until smooth.
5. Return the puréed cauliflower and the reserved pieces to the saucepan. Preheat just until piping hot. Do not boil.
6. Serve topped with additional grated cheese and minced parsley.

End-of-the-Week (or Month) Vegetable Soup

If you have chopped, sliced, or diced vegetables left in the refrigerator as you get to the end of the week and they are losing some of their freshness, use them in the following soup. Even chopped salad greens can go into this soup, and it's delicious. Vegetables that were frozen without blanching for chain cooking start to lose their flavor and texture by the end of a month, so use up these vegetables in this recipe, too. The nice thing about this soup is that it changes flavor from week to week — it's always a surprise.

4–6 SERVINGS

1 pound mixed vegetables
3 cups *Rich Chicken Broth*, **p. 85, or canned broth**
1 tablespoon butter or margarine
3 ounces cheddar cheese
2 ounces leftover boiled, baked, or mashed potato
salt and pepper to taste

1. Cook the vegetables in the chicken broth in a covered 3-quart saucepan until tender (about 20 minutes at most).
2. Put the butter, cheese, and potatoes in a blender container and add the vegetable mixture a little at a time (do not fill the blender more than half full). Purée until smooth.
3. Return the soup to the saucepan and reheat until piping hot. Do not boil.
4. Serve topped with grated cheese if desired.

Fish Chowder

8 LARGE SERVINGS

1½ pounds any type of thick-fleshed fish fillets (cod, haddock, halibut, pike, pickerel, or fresh perch)
1 large bay leaf
1 large onion, diced
2 celery stalks, diced
2 large carrots, diced or sliced
2 tablespoons bacon fat or rendered salt pork fat
4 medium-size potatoes, diced small
2 teaspoons salt
½ teaspoon pepper
¼ teaspoon mace
2 tablespoons minced fresh parsley
4 cups milk or half-and-half

This chowder is best made the day before serving.

1. Cut the fish into 1-inch cubes. Place them in a medium-size saucepan, cover with cold water, and add the bay leaf. Cover the pan, bring the mixture to a boil, remove from the heat, and let stand for 5 minutes. Drain the fish, reserving the stock.

2. Sauté onion, celery, and carrots in bacon fat until they are limp but not brown.

3. Add the potatoes, salt, pepper, mace, and parsley. Cover the vegetables with the reserved fish stock; add water if necessary. Do not add too much stock or water — just barely cover the vegetables.

4. Cover the pan. Bring the mixture to a boil. Reduce the heat and simmer until the potatoes are tender.

5. Add the fish and milk to the pan. Heat to simmering.

6. Cover and let stand for 15 minutes to blend the flavors before serving.

Ground Beef and Pasta Soup

To make this soup without a slow-cooker, cook the beef and broth mixture on top of the stove in a covered saucepan for 1 hour before adding the remaining ingredients. This soup is best made the day before serving. Use your favorite pasta.

6–8 SERVINGS

- 1 cup diced onion
- 1 pound lean ground beef
- 1 tablespoon vegetable oil
- 2 cups canned tomatoes with their juice
- 3 cups beef broth, water, or a combination of the two
- ½ cup diced celery
- 2 tablespoons minced fresh parsley
- ⅛ teaspoon pepper
- 1½ teaspoons salt
- ½ cup pasta, uncooked

1. Sauté the onion and ground beef in oil until the beef loses its pink color.

2. Put the beef mixture in a slow cooker. Add the tomatoes and beef broth. Cover and cook for 6–10 hours (until you are ready to finish making the soup).

3. Pour the beef mixture into a 4-quart saucepan and add the remaining ingredients. Bring to a boil, reduce the heat, and cook, covered, for 20 minutes. Thin with additional broth if the soup is too thick.

Broccoli, Cauliflower, and Cheddar Soup

It's the potatoes that give this soup its thick and creamy texture. It is best made a day ahead of serving.

6–8 SERVINGS

4 cups *Rich Chicken Broth,* p. 85, or canned broth
2 tablespoons butter, margarine, or rendered chicken fat
1 teaspoon onion powder
10 ounces frozen broccoli
10 ounces frozen cauliflower
4 ounces finely diced potato
6 ounces cheddar cheese
½ cup all-purpose cream or half-and-half
salt and pepper to taste

1. Put the broth, butter, onion powder, broccoli, cauliflower, and potato into a 4-quart, heavy saucepan.
2. Cover the pan and bring the mixture to a boil. Reduce the heat and cook for 10 minutes.
3. With a slotted spoon, remove about 1 cup of broccoli and cauliflower pieces and set aside.
4. Re-cover the pan and continue cooking for another 10 minutes.
5. Chop the cheddar cheese into a blender container. Add the cream. Ladle in part of the vegetable-broth mixture. Do not overfill the blender or you may be burned. Purée until the mixture is very smooth. Pour it into a large bowl and continue to purée the vegetable-broth mixture until all the vegetables are puréed.
6. Return the puréed soup to the saucepan along with the reserved vegetables. Reheat just until piping hot. Do not boil or the cheese will curdle and become hard.
7. Add salt and pepper.

Chicken Vegetable Soup

If you prefer a thinner soup, more broth can be added. For the best flavor, be sure to include some onions, carrots, celery, and cabbage among the vegetables.

To save time skip the sautéing in step #1 — just add the broth to the vegetables and fat and continue.

6–8 SERVINGS

- 2 tablespoons butter, margarine or rendered chicken fat
- 4 cups sliced, diced, or chopped vegetables of your choice
- 4 cups *Rich Chicken Broth,* p.85, or canned broth
- 1½ teaspoons dried parsley
- ¼ teaspoon dried celery flakes
- ⅛ teaspoon poultry seasoning
- 1 cup fine noodles
- 1 cup cooked, diced chicken
- salt and pepper to taste

1. Melt the butter in a heavy, 3-quart saucepan. Add the vegetables and sauté for 5 minutes.
2. Add the chicken broth and seasonings. Cover the pan and bring to a boil. Reduce the heat and simmer for 15 minutes.
3. Add the noodles and the chicken. Return to a boil. Then reduce the heat and cook for an additional 10 minutes.
4. Add salt and pepper.

CHAPTER 4
CASSEROLES AND SIDE DISHES

The following group of recipes can be made up all or in part ahead of time and finished at the last minute. Whenever possible, take a few extra minutes and make up at least one extra meal's worth of the recipe to pop in the freezer for another day. Do not add toppings to the dish to be frozen. Cracker or bread crumb toppings can be added at the last minute before the dish is baked.

Super-Quick Spanish Rice with Beef

4 SERVINGS

- ½ **pound lean ground beef**
- ¼ **cup diced onion**
- ½ **cup diced green pepper**
- 1½ **teaspoons vegetable oil**
- 1½ **cups canned tomatoes with juice**
- 1 **cup water**
- ½ **teaspoon salt**
- ⅛ **teaspoon pepper**
- 1½ **cups** *Instant Herbed Rice Mix,* **p. 70**
- 3 **ounces cheddar cheese, grated**

To save even more time, you can stir the cheese into the meat-tomato mixture along with the rice. Cover, let stand for 8 minutes, and serve.

1. Preheat the oven to 375°F.
2. Brown the meat and the onion and green pepper in vegetable oil in a large skillet that has oven-proof handles.
3. When the meat has lost its pink color and the vegetables are tender crisp, add the tomatoes, water, salt, and pepper.
4. Bring the mixture to a boil and stir in the rice mix. Cover and remove from the heat. Let stand for 5 minutes.
5. Top with the grated cheese. Then slip the skillet into the preheated oven and bake until the cheese melts, about 10 minutes.

Slow-Cooker Rice and Vegetable Casserole

4–6 SERVINGS

1 cup long-grained white rice, uncooked
½ cup diced onion
½ cup diced red or green pepper
2 cups cooked whole kernel corn, drained
½ pound ground beef
4 cups tomato juice
2 tablespoons brown sugar
1 teaspoon salt
¼ teaspoon pepper
2 tablespoons rendered bacon fat

This is a very easy casserole to make because it goes together without even precooking the meat. It is a meal in itself, and needs only a salad and beverage to complete it.

If the vegetables are frozen, run them under cold water to defrost and squeeze out the excess moisture.

1. Mix all the ingredients in a slow-cooker.
2. Cover and cook on low (200°F) for 8–10 hours.
3. Uncover the cooker and let the casserole stand for 10 minutes before serving.

Variation:

Cook 4 slices of bacon, use the drippings in the casserole and place the bacon strips over the top of casserole before serving.

If you have a slow-cooker with a removable liner, you can transfer this casserole to a conventional oven set at 375°F for 20 minutes for a more baked taste.

Beefy Rice and Mushrooms

4 SERVINGS

1⅓ cups *Homemade Beef Stock,* p. 86, or canned broth
1⅓ cups *Instant Herbed Rice Mix,* p. 70
½ cup sliced canned mushrooms, drained
½ teaspoon salt (omit with packaged broth)
2 teaspoons butter or margarine

This dish can be made with chicken broth to go with a chicken or fish entrée.

1. Bring the beef broth to a boil in a small saucepan.
2. Add the remaining ingredients and stir well.
3. Cover the pan, remove from the heat, and let stand for 5–7 minutes.

Fried Rice

4–6 SERVINGS

- 4 slices bacon, diced
- ¼ cup diced green pepper
- ¼ cup diced red pepper
- ½ cup diced celery
- 8–10 green onions, sliced thin, or 1 cup diced onion
- ¾ cup cooked, drained mushrooms, or 1 cup diced raw mushrooms
- 4 tablespoons vegetable oil
- 4 cups leftover cooked rice
- ½ teaspooon salt
- ⅛ teaspoon pepper
- 2 teaspoons soy sauce
- 2 teaspoons brown sugar
- 2 eggs
- 1 cup fresh or canned bean sprouts

Use this recipe to make fried rice with leftover cooked brown rice or long-grained white rice.

1. Fry the bacon until crisp in a very large skillet sprayed with vegetable oil. Remove the fried pieces with a slotted spoon and set aside.
2. Over high heat, stir-fry the peppers, celery, onions, and mushrooms in the bacon drippings. Remove with a slotted spoon and set aside.
3. Add the vegetable oil and rice to the pan. Stir-fry the rice for 5 minutes, just until the rice is lightly browned.
4. While the rice is frying, add the salt, pepper, soy sauce, and brown sugar to the eggs and beat lightly in a small bowl.
5. Return the bacon and fried vegetables to the rice. Add the bean sprouts and mix well. Heat for 2 minutes.
6. Push the rice to one side of the pan. Add the egg mixture and cook, stirring constantly. When the egg mixture is almost done, incorporate it into the rice and mix well. Shut off the heat and let the fried rice stand for 5 minutes to blend the flavors. Serve.

Instant Fried Rice

4-6 SERVINGS

½ cup diced green pepper
1 cup diced onion
½ cup diced celery
2 tablespoons bacon drippings, butter, or margarine
1⅓ cups *Instant Herbed Rice Mix*, p. 70
1¼-1½ cups *Homemade Beef Stock*, p. 86, *Rich Chicken Broth*, p. 85, or canned broth

1½ teaspoons soy sauce
2 dashes Chinese hot oil (optional)
1 teaspoon brown sugar
salt and pepper to taste

For a softer rice, add the larger amount of water.

1. Sauté the vegetables in butter, adding a small amount of broth if necessary to keep the vegetables from browning.
2. When the vegetables are tender crisp, add the rice mix, broth, soy sauce, hot oil, and brown sugar. Stir well.
3. Bring the mixture to a boil. Cover the pan, remove from the heat, and let stand for 6 minutes, stirring once after 3 minutes.
4. Season with salt and pepper. Fluff with a fork before serving.

Mashed Potatoes

These potatoes contain an unusual ingredient: baking powder. Its use is optional, but it does make these potatoes lighter and fluffier than regular mashed potatoes.

4 SERVINGS

1 pound potatoes, peeled and boiled
2 tablespoons butter or margarine
¼ cup milk
salt and pepper to taste
¼ teaspoon baking powder (optional)

1. Drain the potatoes thoroughly and return the pan to the heat with the cover cracked for just 30 seconds to dry the potatoes.
2. Heat the milk and butter in a small saucepan or metal measuring cup.
3. Beat the milk into the potatoes with an electric beater until light and fluffy.
4. Sprinkle the baking powder and salt and pepper over the potatoes and beat them in thoroughly. Serve hot.

Slow-Cooker Baked Potatoes

These have got to be the best-flavored baked potatoes I have ever eaten. The potatoes will be crisp on the outside and fluffy inside. If you are going to be away for a long day, bake two very large potatoes instead of four medium-size potatoes — they will not overcook. If you do not have a rack, you can create one with canning jar screw bands, see p. 19.

4 SERVINGS

4 medium-size (5-8-ounce) baking potatoes, well scrubbed

1. Place a wire rack in the bottom of a slow-cooker. Place two sheets of folded paper towels on the rack. Pierce the potatoes with a fork and place them on the paper towels.

2. Cover the potatoes or the top of the cooker with four sheets of paper towels. Put the cover snugly in place. Cook on LOW (200°F) for 6-10 hours. (The potatoes will be done in 6 hours but will keep for 10.)

3. Transfer the potatoes to a cold conventional oven. Set the baking temperature at 450°F. (A hot oven will do, but it is not necessary.)

4. Bake the potatoes for 15 minutes. (If the oven is already hot, bake them for only 8-10 minutes.)

Microwave-to-Oven Baked Potatoes

If you are cooking other foods in the conventional oven at a lower temperature, just cook the potatoes in the microwave oven for a couple of minutes longer before adding them to the conventional oven.

4 SERVINGS

4 large baking potatoes

1. Scrub the potatoes thoroughly and pierce with a fork.
2. Place two sheets of paper towels on the bottom of the microwave oven. Place the potatoes on the paper and cook on high power for 7 minutes.
3. Rotate the position of the potatoes (not necessary if you have a carousel) and turn the potatoes over. Continue cooking on high power for another 7 minutes.
4. Place the potatoes in a cold (or hot) conventional oven. Set the oven temperature at 425°F. and bake the potatoes until they are done, about 20 minutes, depending on the size of the potatoes. Serve.

Scalloped Potatoes

4–6 SERVINGS

4 large potatoes, peeled and sliced thin
1 large onion, peeled and sliced
1 can cream of celery soup
1 tablespoon butter or margarine
⅓ cup milk
⅓ cup ricotta cheese
⅛ teaspoon pepper

1. Preheat the oven to 375°F.
2. Spray a 2-quart Pyrex casserole dish with vegetable oil.
3. Layer the potatoes and onions until all are used.
4. Put the remaining ingredients in a blender container and blend until smooth.
5. Pour the sauce over the potatoes and onions. Move the vegetables slightly with a fork to allow the sauce to go down around the sides.
6. Cover the dish tightly and bake in the preheated oven for 45 minutes.
7. Uncover the dish and continue baking for 30–40 minutes or until the potatoes are fork tender. Add a little milk if the potatoes start to dry out. Serve hot.

Variation — Cheesey Scalloped Potatoes:
Substitute 4 ounces of processed cheese instead of the ricotta cheese. This makes a wonderful buffet party dish.

Slow-Cooker Baked Beans

5–6 SERVINGS

1 pound dried pea beans
5 small whole onions, cut in half
8 tablespoons brown sugar
1 teaspoon dry mustard
salt and pepper to taste
water
½ **pound lean mixed salt pork, diced in ¾-inch cubes**

If your slow-cooker has a removable oven-safe liner, you can finish the beans in a conventional oven for 30 minutes at 375°F.

1. Place the beans in an 8-quart kettle and cover with cold water to 3 times their depth.
2. Cover the pan and bring the water to a boil. Reduce the heat, remove the cover, and cook for 1 hour.
3. Remove the pan from the heat, cover, and let the beans stand overnight in the water. In the morning drain the beans and put them in the slow cooker.
4. Parboil the onions for 7 minutes. Drain and add to the beans. Reserve the cooking liquid.
5. Add the brown sugar, dry mustard, and salt and pepper.
6. Add water to come up just level with the top of the beans. Use the onion liquid as part of the water.
7. Place the diced salt pork on top.
8. Cover the cooker, set on low (200°F.), and cook for 9–12 hours. Serve hot.

Cheddary Ham and Bean Bake

Beans, ham, and cheese can be assembled in a baking dish, covered and refrigerated. The topping mix can be blended and refrigerated in a covered container for up to 24 hours. To bake, shake the topping mixture well, pour it over the bean, ham, and cheese mixture, and bake as directed.

If you want to double this recipe, use a 9x13-inch baking dish and bake for 1 hour.

4–6 SERVINGS

- 10 ounces frozen julienne-style green beans
- 8 ounces diced, fully cooked, smoked ham
- 4 ounces cheddar cheese, grated (1 cup)
- ½ cup *Baking Powder Biscuit Mix*, p. 68
- 1½ cups milk
- ¼ teaspoon dry mustard
- dash pepper
- 2 eggs

1. Preheat the oven to 350°F.
2. Rinse the beans under cold running water to thaw. Drain thoroughly.
3. Spread the beans in an 8-inch square baking dish that has been sprayed with vegetable oil.
4. Layer the ham and then the cheese on top of the beans.
5. Measure the remaining ingredients into a blender container and blend until smooth.
6. Pour the blender contents over the cheese.
7. Bake, uncovered, in the preheated oven for 40–45 minutes or until golden brown.

Mexicali Baked Omelet

3-4 SERVINGS

4 eggs, separated
¼ teaspoon cream of tartar
2 tablespoons water
pepper and salt to taste
3 tablespoons mayonnaise
4 ounces cheddar cheese, grated
1 cup *South of the Border Salsa,* **p. 154, heated to warm**

1. Preheat the oven to 350°F.
2. Beat the egg whites with the cream of tartar in a medium-size bowl until stiff, but not dry.
3. In a second bowl, beat the egg yolks, water, pepper, a sprinkling of salt, and mayonnaise until the mixture is thick and lemon colored.
4. Gently fold the yolks into the whites until no more white is visible (use a wire whisk).
5. Carefully turn the mixture into a large (10-inch) oiled skillet that has straight sides and an oven-proof handle (cast-iron is best).
6. Bake in the preheated oven for 15–20 minutes until the omelet puffs and the top is slightly dry.
7. Top the omelet with grated cheese without removing it from the oven. Continue baking until the cheese has melted, 5–10 minutes.
8. Remove the omelet from the oven. Carefully slide it from the skillet onto a large serving platter.
9. Top with the warm salsa. With a large spatula, carefully fold the omelet in half. Serve immediately.

Crustless Broccoli Quiche

4 SERVINGS

10 ounces frozen broccoli spears or pieces
4 eggs
2 tablespoons grated Parmesan cheese
2 tablespoons milk
4 ounces cheddar cheese, cut in 1-inch chunks
dash cayenne
1 teaspoon onion powder
¼ teaspoon salt (optional)
½ cup diced onion
2 tablespoons butter or margarine

Swiss cheese may be substituted for the cheddar cheese in this dish.

1. Preheat the oven to 350°F.
2. Steam-cook the broccoli for 5 minutes or until tender crisp. Drain well.
3. Put the eggs, Parmesan cheese, milk, cheddar cheese, cayenne, onion powder, and salt in a blender container and blend until smooth.
4. Sauté the diced onion in butter until translucent.
5. Put the onion in a 9-inch Pyrex pie plate sprayed with vegetable oil.
6. Add the drained broccoli to the pie plate and pour the blender contents over it.
7. Bake in the preheated oven for 20 minutes or until a knife inserted half-way between the center and the outer edge comes out clean.
8. Let stand for 5 minutes before serving.

Slow-Cooker Lasagna

If you are going to be away for a long day, prepare the sauce for this recipe the night before. Starting with a cold sauce and using a timed outlet (see p. 13), will give you extra time; otherwise, this dish will be ready in 6 hours. It goes together in minutes since the noodles do not require advance cooking.

8 SERVINGS

1 pound lean ground beef
½ cup diced onion
½ cup diced green pepper
12 ounces tomato paste
2½ cups water
2 teaspoons dried basil
2 teaspoons dried parsley
½ teaspoon garlic powder
¼ teaspoon crushed red pepper
⅛ teaspoon black pepper
3 teaspoons salt
8 ounces lasagna noodles
6 ounces grated mozzarella cheese
1½ cups ricotta cheese
⅓ cup grated Parmesan cheese

1. Sauté the beef and vegetables in a skillet sprayed with vegetable oil.
2. Add the tomato paste, water, and seasonings and bring to a boil. Reduce the heat and simmer for 10 minutes. Stir often.
3. Refrigerate the sauce overnight or go on with the recipe.
4. Spray a 5-quart slow-cooker with vegetable oil.
5. Layer the ingredients as follows:
    - ☐ sauce (Go easy on the sauce until you reach the last layer.)
    - ☐ noodles (Break them up to fill in where necessary, you won't notice it when they are done.)
    - ☐ mozzarella cheese
    - ☐ sauce
    - ☐ noodles
    - ☐ ricotta cheese
    - ☐ sauce
    - ☐ noodles

- ☐ sauce (Use up whatever sauce is left. You should have plenty to cover this layer; do not add extra moisture.)
- ☐ grated Parmesan cheese

6. Set the cooker on low (200°F) and cook for 6 hours (8 hours if started with cold sauce).
7. Remove the cover and let stand for 15 minutes before serving.

Chestnut Stuffing

This stuffing can be baked for 20 minutes in a 350–375°F oven in a covered casserole dish sprayed with vegetable oil. Uncover the casserole dish and continue baking for 10 minutes.

8 HALF-CUP SERVINGS

½ pound country-style pork sausage
12 peeled and chopped chestnuts (see p. 25)
½ cup diced onion
½ cup diced celery
1 cup chicken broth or water
3 cups breadcrumbs from *Homemade Stuffing Bread*, p. 76

1. Sauté the sausage in a large, heavy skillet sprayed with vegetable oil, until it loses its pink color. Drain off the excess fat, reserving 2 tablespoons.
2. Return the fat to the pan with the sausage, chestnuts, and vegetables.
3. Sauté the vegetables until they are tender crisp. Add a small amount of chicken broth if necessary to keep the vegetables from browning.
4. Add 1 cup chicken broth or water. Bring to a boil and then turn off the heat.
5. Stir in the stuffing crumbs.
6. Let stand for 5 minutes before stuffing the poultry.

Pizza

This pizza crust is better tasting than anything you can purchase from the frozen-food case or a take-out restaurant, and it takes just minutes to prepare. In fact, you can't go to the store, buy a pizza, and bake it any faster than you can make this one right at home.

4–6 SERVINGS

- 2 cups *Homemade Bread Mix* (p. 63), stirred well before measuring
- 1 package quick-rising dry yeast
- ½ teaspoon dried basil
- ¼ teaspoon garlic powder
- 2 teaspoons vegetable oil
- ½–¾ cup very hot tap water (120–130°F.)
- 3 ounces tomato paste
- 6 tablespoons water
- 1 teaspoon dried basil
- dash garlic powder (or to taste)
- dash salt
- 1 teaspoon vegetable oil
- 2 ounces cheddar cheese, grated
- 3 ounces mozzarella cheese
- 3 ounces thin-sliced pepperoni, cooked sausage or ground beef
- ½ cup diced onion, peppers, and mushrooms combined (optional)

1. Preheat the oven to 450°F.
2. Measure the bread mix, yeast, seasonings, and oil into a food processor bowl fitted with a steel chopping blade. Put the cover in place.
3. With the processor running, slowly pour the hot tap water through the feed tube until the mixture forms a ball that leaves the sides of the bowl. Let the ball revolve in the bowl 35 times. Let the dough remain in the food processor with the cover on for 10 minutes.
4. Remove the dough from the processor, knead it 10–15 times, and immediately roll it out to fit a 14-inch pizza pan or a 10x15-inch baking sheet with 1-inch sides.
5. Fit the dough into the pan, pinching the edges here and there over the side of the pan to keep the dough from shrinking.
6. Put the crust in the preheated oven and bake for 5 minutes.
7. While the dough is baking, mix the tomato paste, water, and seasonings thoroughly. Set aside.
8. Remove the partially baked crust from the oven. Brush the crust with 1 teaspoon vegetable oil.

9. Spread the sauce over the oiled crust, sprinkle with grated Parmesan cheese, top with cheddar and mozzarella, and add the sliced pepperoni and vegetables.

10. Return the pizza to the oven and bake for an additional 8–12 minutes or until all the cheese has melted and is bubbly, and the vegetables are cooked (without the vegetables it takes only 8–10 minutes).

11. Let the pizza stand for 1 minute before slicing to allow the cheese to set.

Variations:

Try making this pizza with just one kind of cheese.

Crusts may be made up through step #8 and frozen. To finish, simply complete the steps as directed, allowing a few extra minutes of baking time for the frozen crust. If you are making several crusts, take the dough out of the processor in step #3 and put it in an oiled bowl. Cover lightly and proceed as directed.

Baked Cheese and Onion Fondue

6 SERVINGS

8 slices day-old bread
2 large onions, sliced very thin
2 tablespoons butter
6 ounces Swiss cheese, thinly sliced
4 eggs
2½ cups milk
1½ teaspoons salt
½ teaspoon prepared mustard
¼ teaspoon pepper
dash cayenne
dash paprika
2 tablespoons minced fresh parsley

This dish must be refrigerated for at least 8 hours (and up to 24 hours) before baking.

1. Trim the crust from 4 slices of the bread; reserve the trimmings.
2. Cut the remaining slices of bread into large cubes.
3. Sauté the onions in butter until they are limp but not brown.
4. Layer the cubes of bread and the bread crusts with the cheese and onions in a 9-inch Pyrex baking dish, sprayed with vegetable oil.
5. Top with the remaining 4 slices of bread.
6. Put the eggs, milk, salt, mustard, and peppers in a blender container and blend until smooth. Pour over the bread mixture.
7. Cover the dish tightly with plastic wrap and refrigerate for at least 8 hours or up to 24 hours.
8. Preheat the oven to 375°F.
9. Sprinkle with paprika and parsley before baking.
10. Bake in a 375°F. oven for 45–55 minutes or until puffed and golden brown on top.
11. Let stand for 10 minutes before serving.

CHAPTER 5
FISH

Overnight Crabmeat Casserole

This dish must be prepared a day in advance and refrigerated for 24 hours before baking.

4 SERVINGS

2 tablespoons mayonnaise
8 slices whole wheat or white bread, crusts trimmed
6½ ounces canned, drained crabmeat, cartilage removed
salt
2 cups milk
4 eggs
8 ounces cheddar cheese, grated

1. Spray a 9-inch square Pyrex baking dish with vegetable oil.
2. Spread the mayonnaise on one side of 4 slices of the trimmed bread. Place the bread in the baking dish with the mayonnaise side up.
3. Spread the crabmeat over the bread. Salt lightly.
4. Measure the milk and eggs into a blender container. Blend until smooth.
5. Pour the blender contents over the crabmeat. Top with the cheddar cheese.
6. Lay the last 4 slices of bread over the cheese.
7. Cover the dish tightly with plastic wrap and refrigerate for about 24 hours.
8. Preheat the oven to 350°F.
9. Bake in the preheated oven for 45 minutes.
10. Let stand for 5 minutes before serving.

Baked Cod with Shrimp Sauce

This entrée takes less than a half-hour to prepare. It is so pretty and so delicious, you will want to serve it often. I've heard friends say that they don't like baked fish because it is too dry. However, the problem is more often with the cook than the fish. When fish is overcooked, it loses all of its moisture and flavor. Fish fillets from 1 to 1½ inches thick should be baked at 350°F for no more than 20–25 minutes. Add 10 minutes for frozen fillets.

4 SERVINGS

1½ pounds thick fish fillets, cut in serving-size pieces
1 slice bread
1½ teaspoons butter or margarine
¼ teaspoon dry lemon zest
½ can cream of shrimp soup
2 tablespoons water
2 ounces Velveeta® cheese
dash garlic powder
dash hot pepper sauce (optional)
minced fresh parsley
paprika

1. Preheat the oven to 350°F.
2. Rinse the fish fillets and pat dry. Place them in a 9-inch Pyrex baking dish sprayed with vegetable oil.
3. Spread the bread with butter. Fold it in half and break it up into a blender container. Add the lemon zest.
4. Run the blender on high to crumb the bread. Pour the crumbs onto a piece of wax paper and set aside.
5. Measure the soup, water, cheese, garlic powder, and hot sauce into the blender container. Purée until smooth.
6. Pour the sauce over the fish fillets. Top with the bread crumb mixture. Sprinkle parsley and paprika over all.
7. Bake in the preheated oven for 20–25 minutes, or until the fish flakes easily with a fork.

Baked Stuffed Fillet of Sole

4 SERVINGS

¼ cup diced onion
¼ cup diced celery
¼ cup diced, canned mushrooms
1 tablespoon butter or margarine
6 tablespooons *Rich Chicken Broth*, p. 85, or canned broth
¾ cup *Homemade Stuffing Breadcrumbs*, p. 76
1½ pounds fillet of sole, cut in large serving pieces
1 can cream of chicken soup
1 teaspoon grated fresh lemon peel
2 tablespoons finely minced fresh parsley
paprika

This recipe may be prepared up to 24 hours in advance and covered and refrigerated until baking time. Add 10 minutes to the baking time.

1. Preheat the oven to 350°F.
2. Sauté the vegetables in butter until they are tender and the juices have evaporated.
3. Add the vegetables and 4 tablespoons chicken broth to the stuffing crumbs and mix well. Then let stand for 5 minutes.
4. Rinse the fish and pat it dry.
5. Put a spoonful of stuffing in the center of each fillet. Roll the fillet around the stuffing.
6. Put the fish rolls, seam-side down, in a baking dish sprayed with vegetable oil.
7. Blend the cream of chicken soup with the remaining chicken broth until smooth. Pour the sauce over the fish rolls.
8. Sprinkle the lemon peel, parsley, and paprika over all.
9. Bake, uncovered, in the preheated oven for 25 minutes.

Salmon Ring

This delicious molded pâté could not be easier to make. To unmold molded salads, turn the mold upside down onto a serving plate; wet a large towel with very hot water and wring it out; wrap the towel around the mold for 1-2 minutes, pressing it against the sides of the mold. Lift off the mold. If the mold offers resistance, loosen the edges with a table knife and try again.

12-15 HORS D'OEUVRE SERVINGS

- **2 packages unflavored gelatin**
- **¼ cup cold water**
- **1 can cream of mushroom soup**
- **1 8-ounce package cream cheese**
- **1 16-ounce can pink or red salmon, drained**
- **½ cup diced onion**
- **½ cup diced celery**

1. Mix the gelatin with the cold water. Let it stand for 1 minute to dissolve.
2. Heat the cream of mushroom soup in a small saucepan, stirring constantly.
3. Add the gelatin mixture to the soup. Continue to heat until the gelatin dissolves. Do not boil.
4. Pour the soup-gelatin mixture into a blender container. Add the cheese and the drained salmon.
5. Blend until smooth. Stir in the onions and celery.
6. Pour into a 6-cup mold sprayed with vegetable oil.
7. Chill for several hours until firm. Serve with crackers.

Never-Fail Seafood Newburg

This recipe is actually a low-calorie version of Lobster Newburg. It is so quick and easy to prepare, in addition to the fact that it never fails, that you must make it to believe it. I will challenge any Newburg recipe to taste better. Use young and tender zucchini and real butter. You must peel the zucchini to avoid a green Newburg.

The poaching liquid can be saved for fish chowder or discarded.

4 SERVINGS

1 pound any mixture of shellfish or thick-fleshed fish fillets, cut in 1-inch chunks
chicken broth, fish stock, or water to cover fish
6 ounces peeled, but *not* seeded, raw zucchini, cut in chunks
1 ounce diced onion
dash white pepper
⅔ cup *Rich Chicken Broth*, p. 85, or canned broth
1 tablespoon butter
6 ounces Velveeta® cheese
1 ounce grated Parmesan cheese
¼ cup cooking sherry
3 ounces boiled potato
dash cayenne

1. Put the fish pieces in a skillet or saucepan and cover with chicken broth, fish stock, or water and a little salt. Cover the pan and bring to a boil. Then remove from the heat and let stand, covered, for 5–8 minutes.

2. Cook the zucchini, onion, and pepper in the ⅔ cup chicken broth in a covered 1-quart saucepan until the zucchini is mushy.

3. Pour the zucchini mixture into a blender container with the remaining ingredients. Purée until very smooth.

4. Pour the blender contents back into the saucepan. Heat through until the sauce reaches the simmering point, stirring constantly (about 5 minutes).

5. Add the cooked fish and heat through. Do not boil.

Hot Tuna Tacos

4 SERVINGS

12 ounces drained tuna (2 6-ounce cans)
¼ cup diced onion
2 tablespoons diced green pepper or hot chili peppers
¼ cup diced celery
mayonnaise
salt and pepper to taste
8 crisp taco shells
12 ounces Monterey Jack cheese, grated

1. Preheat the oven to 375°F.
2. Mix the tuna, onion, peppers, and celery with enough mayonnaise to moisten.
3. Season with salt and pepper.
4. Fill the taco shells. Put the shells in a 5½x13-inch baking dish sprayed with vegetable oil. Top with the grated cheese.
5. Bake in the preheated oven for about 15 minutes until the tacos are heated through and the cheese has melted. Serve.

Baked Oriental Fish

4 SERVINGS

1½ pounds thick-fleshed fish fillets, cut in serving-size pieces
1 teaspoon cornstarch
salt
pepper
⅛ teaspoon garlic powder
½ teaspoon ground ginger
½ cup orange marmalade
1 tablespoon soy sauce

This dish may be prepared up to 24 hours in advance and refrigerated until baking time. Add 5-10 minutes to the baking time.

1. Preheat the oven to 350°F.
2. Rinse the fish and pat it dry.
3. Put the fish pieces in a 9-inch Pyrex baking dish sprayed with vegetable oil.
4. Mix the remaining ingredients and pour over the fish.
5. Bake, uncovered, in the preheated oven for 20 minutes or until the thickest pieces flake with a fork. Do not overbake. Serve hot.

Scallops with Linguine

6 SERVINGS

1 pound small bay scallops or large scallops cut in quarters
2 tablespoons lemon juice
1 garlic clove, minced
1 tablespoon chopped fresh parsley
½ teaspoon dill weed
½ teaspoon salt
¼ teaspoon pepper
8 ounces linguine noodles
2 tablespoons butter or margarine
1 can cream of celery soup
grated Parmesan cheese (optional)

1. Marinate the scallops in the lemon juice, garlic, parsley, dill weed, salt, and pepper for 15 minutes to blend the flavors.
2. Cook the linguine according to the package directions. Drain and keep warm.
3. Melt the butter in a skillet and sauté the scallops with their marinade.
4. Drain the juices into a blender container. Add the soup and blend until smooth.
5. Pour the blender contents back into the skillet with the scallops. Reheat just until heated through.
6. Place the linguine on a large platter. Top with the scallop sauce. Sprinkle with grated Parmesan cheese, if desired.

Magic Crust Seafood Pie

6–8 SERVINGS

6 ounces fresh or frozen seafood, cooked
⅓ cup thinly sliced scallions
4 ounces Swiss cheese, grated (1 cup)
½ teaspoon dried basil
¼ teaspoon garlic powder
dash cayenne
1½ cups milk
3 eggs
¾ cup *Baking Powder Biscuit Mix*, p. 68
½ teaspoon salt
⅛ teaspoon black pepper

1. Preheat the oven to 400°F.
2. Spread the seafood, scallions, and cheese in a 10x1½-inch deep-dish pie plate sprayed with vegetable oil.
3. Place the remaining ingredients in a blender container and blend until smooth.
4. Pour over the seafood mixture.
5. Bake in the preheated oven for 30–35 minutes or until a knife inserted in the center of the pie comes out clean.
6. Cool for 5 minutes before serving.

CHAPTER 6
POULTRY

Oven Fried Chicken

This dish couldn't be simpler. The chicken may be coated up to 24 hours beforehand, refrigerated, and popped into the oven when you get home from work. The coating will be wet and less visible, but it will have the same crisping effect.

4 SERVINGS

- **1** 2½-pound frying chicken, cut in pieces
- **1 cup** *Fried Chicken Coating Mix*, p. 64

1. Preheat the oven to 375°F.
2. Rinse the chicken and pat it dry.
3. Put the seasoned coating mix in a plastic bag and shake the chicken in the mix to coat it lightly.
4. Place the chicken, skin-side down, on a cookie sheet with ½–1-inch sides that has been sprayed with vegetable oil.
5. Bake in the preheated oven for 30 minutes.
6. Turn the chicken and continue baking for 20–30 minutes, depending on how thick the pieces are.

Fried Chicken

If you want to parboil the chicken one day and fry it the next, drain the chicken after it has cooled. Refrigerate it in a covered container overnight. Freeze the reserved broth.

If you like thick-coated, extra-crispy chicken, dip it twice in the coating mix.

4 SERVINGS

1 2½-pound frying chicken, cut in pieces
approximately 4 cups chicken broth
1 egg
¼ cup milk
1 cup *Fried Chicken Coating Mix*, p. 64, or more as needed
approximately 1 quart peanut oil or other vegetable oil

1. Put the chicken pieces in an 8-quart covered saucepan. Cover with chicken broth.
2. Cover the pan, bring to a boil, and reduce the heat. Simmer for 10 minutes.
3. Turn off the heat and leave the chicken in the broth until you are ready to fry it.
4. When you are ready to fry, drain the chicken well, reserving the broth for soup, gravy, or sauces.
5. Put the egg and milk in a blender container and blend until smooth. Pour into a shallow dish.
6. Put the **Chicken Coating Mix** in a shallow bowl or plastic bag.
7. Heat 1½ inches of oil in a deep heavy skillet to 385°F.
8. Pat dry the drained chicken with paper towels. Dip the chicken in the egg-milk mixture and shake off the excess. Coat with the coating mix and shake off the excess.
9. Fry the chicken in the heated oil until golden brown on both sides. Do not overcrowd the chicken in the pan if you want crispy chicken.

10. Drain the cooked chicken on paper towels. Keep it warm in the oven (or low) until serving.

Stir-Fried Chicken and Vegetables

4 SERVINGS

- 2 whole chicken breasts, skinned and boned
- 2 tablespoons rendered chicken fat, butter, or margarine
- 3 cups thin-sliced mixed fresh vegetables of your choice
- ½ cup *Rich Chicken Broth,* p. 85, or canned broth
- 1½ teaspoons cornstarch
- 1 tablespoon soy sauce
- 1 tablespoon cooking sherry (optional)
- ¼ teaspoon garlic powder
- ½ teaspoon finely minced fresh ginger, or a couple dashes Chinese hot oil
- 1 teaspoon brown sugar

1. Dice or slice the chicken in small pieces.
2. Melt the butter in a heavy skillet or wok. When the skillet is hot, add the chicken and the vegetables.
3. Stir-fry the chicken and vegetables until the chicken is tender and the vegetables are tender crisp. Do not overcook.
4. Mix the remaining ingredients in a small bowl.
5. Stir the sauce into the vegetables, stirring constantly. When the mixture comes to a boil, simmer for 1 minute. Serve immediately.

Slow-Cooker Roast Chicken

You must have a 4½-quart or larger slow-cooker for this recipe. Bake some potatoes in a second slow-cooker, and you will have a complete roast chicken dinner ready when you come home from work. If you want to stuff the chicken, reduce the amount of broth in the stuffing by ¼ cup; otherwise, the condensation from the slow-cooker will make it too moist.

4–6 SERVINGS

1 3½–4½-pound roasting chicken
2 cups stuffing; see *Homemade Bread Stuffing*, p. 76 (optional)
salt and pepper
paprika

1. Rinse the chicken thoroughly inside and out and pat it dry.
2. Stuff if desired.
3. Sprinkle lightly with salt and pepper, and rub paprika over all.
4. Place a round rack in the bottom of the slow-cooker and place the chicken on the rack. Cover the top of the cooker with four sheets of paper towel. Put the cover snugly in place. Cook on low (200°F.) for 8–10 hours.
5. If you want the cooked chicken to have a crispy brown skin, carefully transfer it to a small roasting pan (or leave it in the removable crockery liner) and place it in a *cold* oven. Set the oven temperature to 375°F. and roast for 20 minutes. The chicken will be nice and moist inside with crispy brown skin outside.
6. Let the chicken stand for 15 minutes before serving to allow the juices to set and to make carving easier.

Variation:
For an extra special treat, baste the chicken with melted grape jelly while it is finishing in the oven, but then don't add the slow-cooker juices to the roasting pan when making gravy.

Roast Duckling with Brandied Apricot Sauce

This duckling may be preroasted up to the point of basting and then refrigerated overnight. To serve, preheat the oven, heat the sauce, baste the duckling, and proceed, roasting 15-20 minutes longer than the half hour called for.

4 SERVINGS

1 4-5-pound duckling, quartered
¼ cup all-purpose flour
salt
pepper
garlic powder
1⅞ cups apricot preserves
1 cup apricot brandy
salt
cayenne
½ teaspoon garlic powder

1. Preheat the oven to 375°F.
2. Wash the duckling pieces and pat them dry.
3. Put the flour in a plastic bag with a light sprinkling of salt, pepper, and garlic powder. Shake the duckling pieces, one at a time, in the flour mixture. Shake off the excess.
4. Place the duckling, skin side up, on a wire rack set in a *deep* roasting pan. (Otherwise, fat will spatter the oven.)
5. Roast in the preheated oven for 1½ hours. Then remove from the oven and drain off the fat.
6. Remove the wire rack from the pan and return the duckling to the pan, skin-side up.
7. While the duckling is roasting, make the sauce. Measure the apricot preserves, brandy, a dash of salt, dash of cayenne, and the garlic powder into a blender container and blend until smooth.
8. Heat the sauce in a small saucepan until just heated through.
9. Baste the drained duckling with the heated sauce and return it to the oven. Continue roasting for another ½ hour, basting every 10 minutes with the sauce.

Slow-Cooker New-Fashioned Boiled Dinner

Meat dishes with uncooked vegetables take as much as 4 hours longer to cook in a slow-cooker than meat dishes without vegetables. However, on the top of the stove, vegetables cook very quickly. In this dish the meat will cook long and slow in the slow-cooker, and then the vegetables will be cooked in the broth on top of the stove in just 20–25 minutes.

Frying chickens have less flavor than roasting chickens, so if you use a frying chicken, cook it in broth instead of water.

4–6 SERVINGS

1 3½-pound frying or roasting chicken
water or chicken broth to cover
2 teaspoons salt (omit with canned broth)
⅛ teaspoon pepper
½ teaspoon onion powder
1 medium-size head cabbage, cut in 6 wedges
1 pound carrots, cut in medium-thick chunks
6 medium-size potatoes, peeled and halved
6 medium-size onions, peeled

1. Place the chicken, broth, 1 teaspoon salt, pepper, and onion powder in a slow-cooker. Cover and cook on low (200°F.) for 8–10 hours.

2. Pour off the broth into a large covered kettle. Leave the chicken in the covered slow-cooker on warm.

3. Add the vegetables to the broth with the remaining 1 teaspoon salt. Cover the kettle, bring to a boil, and simmer until the vegetables are tender, about 20 minutes.

4. Place the warm chicken in the center of a large platter, surround it with the vegetables, and serve. Ladle the extra broth into a bowl to be served with the vegetables.

Variation:
Traditionally, the boiled dinner has been made with ham, corned beef, or short ribs of beef, and you can certainly use those meats in this recipe if you wish — the timing will be the same. However, with everyone so conscious of the dangers of excess fat and cholesterol in our diets, it is only common

Variation, continued:

sense to try this dish with chicken. The results are well worth it. Chicken is usually less expensive than the other cuts of meat, so it is a cost-conscious recipe, as well.

Slow-Cooker Fricassee of Chicken

4 SERVINGS

¼ cup diced onion
¼ cup diced celery
¼ cup diced carrot
2 tablespoons butter or margarine
1 can cream of chicken soup
¼ teaspoon poultry seasoning
1 teaspoon dried parsley
1 2½-pound frying chicken, cut in pieces

1. Sauté the onion, celery, and carrot in butter until tender. Do not brown.
2. Put the sautéed vegetables in a blender container with the chicken soup and poultry seasoning. Blend until smooth.
3. Stir in the parsley.
4. Rinse the chicken pieces and pat them dry.
5. Place the chicken in a slow-cooker and cover with the soup mixture. Do not add water. Cover the cooker and cook on low (200°F.) for 8 hours.

Chicken Pot Pie

4–6 SERVINGS

⅓ cup butter or margarine
⅓ cup diced onion
1 tablespoon parsley
⅓ cup diced celery
1⅓ cups *Baking Powder Biscuit Mix,* p. 68
½ teaspoon salt
⅛ teaspoon pepper
¾ cup milk
1½ cups *Rich Chicken Broth,* p. 85, or gravy
2 cups diced, cooked chicken
2 cups frozen peas and carrots
½ teaspoon poultry seasoning

Turkey or rabbit may be substituted for the chicken in this recipe.

1. Preheat the oven to 425°F.
2. Heat the butter in a medium-size saucepan until it is melted.
3. Sauté the onion, parsley, and celery just until tender.
4. Mix in ⅓ cup of the biscuit mix and the salt and pepper. Cook over a low heat, stirring constantly, until the mixture is bubbly.
5. Combine ½ cup of the milk with the chicken broth or gravy. Stir into the vegetable mixture and heat to boiling, stirring constantly. Boil for 1 minute.
6. Stir in the chicken and frozen vegetables. Cook until heated through.
7. Mix the remaining 1 cup of biscuit mix with the remaining ¼ cup of milk and the poultry seasoning until a soft dough forms.
8. Turn the dough out onto a floured board and knead 6–7 times until it is smooth. Roll the dough into an 8-inch circle.
9. Pour the chicken mixture into a 2-quart, round casserole dish sprayed with vegetable oil.
10. Top with the dough. Cut slits in the center to allow steam to escape.
11. Bake, uncovered, in the preheated oven until the top is light brown, 15–20 minutes.

Super-Quick Turkey Divan

This dish can be prepared 24 hours ahead and refrigerated until baking time. Chicken or rabbit may be substituted for the turkey in this recipe.

6 SERVINGS

- 20 ounces frozen broccoli spears
- 2 ounces cheddar cheese, grated (½ cup)
- 12 ounces sliced, cooked turkey
- ¼ cup milk
- ¼ teaspoon nutmeg
- 1 10¾-ounce can cream of chicken soup
- 1 cup *Baking Powder Biscuit Mix,* p. 68
- ¼ cup cold butter or margarine, cut in chunks
- 2 tablespoons grated Parmesan cheese
- paprika

1. Preheat the oven to 400°F.
2. Rinse the broccoli under cold running water to thaw. Drain thoroughly.
3. Arrange the broccoli in an 11x7x1½ baking dish sprayed with vegetable oil.
4. Sprinkle the grated cheddar cheese over the broccoli.
5. Layer the turkey slices over the cheese.
6. Blend the milk, nutmeg, and soup and pour over the turkey.
7. Measure the biscuit mix into a food processor bowl fitted with a steel cutting blade, add the butter and Parmesan cheese and process until crumbly. Sprinkle over the soup mixture.
8. Top with paprika.
9. Bake, uncovered, in the preheated oven until golden brown, about 25 minutes.

Chicken Divan Quickie

For a crispy topping, add some buttered breadcrumbs (p. 76) to the top of the cheese before broiling. Cheddar cheese may be substituted for the Swiss cheese.

4 SERVINGS

¾ pound chicken, boned and skinned, or ½ pound sliced, cooked chicken
2 tablespoons vegetable oil
1 cup *Rich Chicken Broth*, p. 85, or canned broth
2 tablespoons cooking sherry
10 ounces frozen broccoli florets
1 can cream of chicken soup

1. Preheat the broiler.
2. Sauté the chicken pieces in the vegetable oil in a large, heavy skillet until cooked, about 5 minutes.
3. Add the broth, sherry, broccoli, and soup to the chicken in the skillet.
4. Bring the mixture to a boil and stir in the rice. Cover and remove from the heat. Let stand for 5 minutes.
5. Top with the cheese and put under the broiler until the cheese melts. Serve.

Holiday Turkey Pie

To prepare this dish in advance, refrigerate the turkey-vegetable mixture and the topping separately. Before baking, assemble as directed and bake. (Make sure to shake the topping mixture well before pouring it over the turkey mixture.) Chicken or rabbit may be substituted for the turkey in this recipe.

6 SERVINGS

2 cups diced, cooked turkey
½ cup diced onion
1 cup diced celery
2 tablespoons minced fresh parsley, or 2 teaspoons dried
½ cup chopped roasted chestnuts (optional)
¾ teaspoon ground sage
¾ teaspoon dried thyme
½ teaspoon poultry seasoning
⅛ teaspoon pepper
½ teaspoon salt
1¼ cups milk
3 eggs
1 cup *Baking Powder Biscuit Mix*, p. 68

1. Preheat the oven to 400°F.
2. Mix the turkey, onion, celery, parsley, chestnuts, and seasonings in a bowl.
3. Turn the mixture into a 10x1½-inch, deep-dish pie plate sprayed with vegetable oil.
4. Measure the remaining ingredients into a blender container and blend until smooth.
5. Pour over the turkey mixture.
6. Bake in the preheated oven for 25–30 minutes or until a knife inserted in the center comes out clean.
7. Cool for 5 minutes before serving.

CHAPTER 7
BEEF, PORK, and LAMB

Slow-Cooker Beef Stroganoff

Hot, buttered noodles and a fresh vegetable salad can be made at the last minute to complete this easy and delicious entrée.

6 SERVINGS

- 2 pounds lean stew beef
- 2 tablespoons butter or margarine
- ¾ cup onion
- 1 large garlic clove, minced
- 2 tablespoons ketchup
- 2 tablespoons minced parsley
- 1 can cream of mushroom soup
- ½ cup sour cream
- 2 tablespoons cooking sherry
- ½ cup sliced, canned mushrooms, drained
- salt and pepper to taste

1. Brown the beef in the butter. Add the onion and garlic and cook for 2 minutes.
2. Put the beef mixture in a slow-cooker.
3. Measure the ketchup, parsley, and soup into a blender container and blend until smooth. Pour over the beef mixture.
4. Cover the cooker and cook on low (200°F.) for 8–10 hours.
5. Stir in the sour cream, sherry, and mushrooms. Turn the heat to high and cook just long enough to heat through.
6. Add salt and pepper. Serve.

Slow-Cooker Prime Rib Roast of Beef

A very large prime rib can be roasted in a conventional oven at 200°F., for 1 hour per pound. You can place a refrigerator-cold, 8-pound roast in your timed oven to start in 2 hours, and it will be ready in 10 hours (8 + 2. See p. 13 for a discussion of timed outlets.) A roast cooks faster in the oven than in a slow-cooker even though the temperature is the same, because of the dry heat that surrounds the roast and evaporates the moisture.

6–8 SERVINGS

1 4-pound, boned and rolled eye-of-the-rib of beef
pepper

1. Brown the roast well on all sides in a hot, lightly oiled skillet. This takes about 10 minutes. Deglaze the pan and store the pan juices in a covered container in the refrigerator.

2. Place the roast on a rack in a slow-cooker. (The rack should be at least 1 inch from the bottom of the cooker.) Sprinkle the roast lightly with pepper. Place 3–4 sheets of paper towel over the top of the slow-cooker; then put the cover snugly in place.

3. Roast on low (200°F.) for 6 hours for rare, 7 hours for medium, and 8 hours for well done.

4. Remove the cover and let the roast stand for 15 minutes before carving.

5. Add the juice from the slow-cooker to the reserved pan juices and heat in a small saucepan for *au jus* gravy. Season to taste.

Big-Batch Meatballs

You can serve these meatballs with spaghetti sauce (p. 157) or cocktail sauce (p. 158). If you want to plan ahead for spaghetti, add the Italian seasonings listed in the Variation at the end of this recipe. If you make seasoned and unseasoned meatballs at the same time, be careful to keep them separate, or you won't be able to tell which ones are which.

100 MEATBALLS

5 pounds lean ground beef
3 eggs
1½ cups quick-cooking oatmeal
2 large onions, diced
1 tablespoon salt
¾ teaspoon pepper

1. Preheat the oven to 400°F.
2. Place the beef in a large bowl.
3. Measure the eggs, oatmeal, onions, salt, and pepper into a blender container and blend until smooth.
4. Pour the blender contents over the beef and mix in well. Use your hands if necessary.
5. Shape the meat into 1-inch balls.
6. Bake in the preheated oven for 20 minutes.
7. Pour off any fat from the baking sheets before using in a sauce or freezing

To freeze: Cool the meatballs at room temperature for 30 minutes before tray freezing. When they are frozen, pack loosely in food-safe freezer bags. Label and use as needed.

Variation:
To make 50 Italian meatballs (half of the recipe), add 1 teaspoon garlic powder, ¾ teaspoon dried oregano, 1 tablespoon dried basil, 1 teaspoon crushed red pepper, and ⅓ cup grated Parmesan cheese to one-half of the meat mixture and blend well.

Pot Roast with Vegetable Gravy

This is a recipe that is set up for quantity cooking. One portion can be used for dinner the night it is made, and the remainder can be frozen in meal-size portions for several more quick-and-easy meals. The frozen vegetable gravy reheats very smoothly, unlike gravies that are made with flour.

20–24 SERVINGS

- 8–10 pounds boneless beef roast (chuck, rump, top or bottom round, eye-of-the-round, or sirloin tip roast beef)
- 2 large onions, cut in chunks
- 4 large carrots, cut in chunks
- 2 medium-size potatoes, cut in chunks
- 1 large celery rib, cut in chunks
- 2 sprigs parsley
- 1 tablespoon Worcestershire sauce
- dash garlic powder
- 8 ounces tomato sauce
- 2 cups water or beef broth
- salt and pepper to taste

1. Wipe the roast with a damp paper towel and put it in a covered roaster.
2. Add the remaining ingredients.
3. Cover tightly and roast at 200°F. for 10 hours. (The oven does not have to be preheated.)
4. Remove the roast from the roasting pan and set it aside, lightly covered to prevent drying.
5. Put the vegetables and the broth in a blender container a little at a time (do not put more than 2 cups in at one time). Purée until smooth. Pour into a large bowl as you go along.
6. Return all the broth to the roaster and reheat to blend. Stir constantly. Serve.

To Freeze: allow the roast to cool slightly. Then slice into serving-size pieces, divide into meal-size portions, place in freezer containers, and cover with gravy. Seal, label, and date the containers. Cool in refrigerator before freezing.

Variation:
If you prefer a thicker gravy, thicken just before serving by pouring the heated gravy into the blender container and adding ½ tablespoon of flour per cup of gravy. Blend thoroughly; then reheat, stirring constantly, until boiling. Reduce the heat and cook for 1 full minute.

Last Minute Stir-Fry

Keep 16-ounce bags of frozen mixed vegetables and stir-fry sauce (p. 155) on hand all the time. Anytime you are caught short for a quick dinner, pick up ½ pound of ground beef on your way home and make this dish. It takes less than 15 minutes. You can even throw together some **Instant Fried Rice** (p. 101) in the same length of time. Try a few diced or sliced onions or fresh bean sprouts in this recipe.

4–6 SERVINGS

½ pound lean ground beef
16 ounces frozen mixed vegetables (broccoli, green beans, peppers, and mushrooms)
1-1½ cups *Sauce for Stir-Fried Dishes,* **p. 155**

1. Sauté the ground beef in a large oiled skillet just until it starts to lose its pink color.
2. Add the frozen vegetables to the skillet. Stir-fry until they are tender crisp.
3. Shake the sauce well to mix. Pour 1–1½ cups sauce into the beef-vegetable mixture, stirring constantly.
4. Bring to a boil. Then reduce the heat and simmer for 1 minute.
5. Adjust the seasonings. Serve immediately.

Slow-Cooker Beef Stew

4–6 SERVINGS

- 1½ pounds lean beef, cut into 1-inch cubes
- 2 tablespoons bacon drippings or vegetable oil
- 2 cups carrots, cut in 1-inch chunks
- 6 small onions
- ½ cup diced celery
- 4 medium-size potatoes, cut in 1-inch cubes
- ½ cup hot water
- 1 can cream of mushroom soup
- 1 1-ounce package dry onion soup mix
- 2 teaspoons Worcestershire sauce
- 1 tablespoon minced fresh parsley
- ⅛ teaspoon pepper
- 1 tablespoon tomato paste

1. Trim the beef well. Brown it in the bacon drippings in a large, heavy skillet.
2. With a slotted spoon, remove the beef and set it aside.
3. Put the carrots, onions, celery, and potatoes in the skillet. Add ½ cup hot water. Cover, bring to a boil and then simmer for 5 minutes.
4. Transfer the vegetables to the bottom of a slow-cooker and add the beef.
5. Mix the remaining ingredients well. Pour over the meat and vegetables. Put the cover in place.
6. Cook on low (200°F.) for 8–10 hours.

Stir-Fried Beef and Snowpeas

4 SERVINGS

- 2 tablespoons peanut oil or vegetable oil
- 1 pound top round steak, sliced in thin strips
- 2 6-ounce packages frozen snow peas
- ½ cup slivered blanched almonds
- 1 tablespoon soy sauce
- 2 tablespoons cooking sherry (optional)
- 1½ cups *Homemade Beef Stock,* p. 86, or canned broth
- 1½ tablespoons cornstarch
- 1 teaspoon brown sugar
- salt and pepper to taste

You can place the beef in a freezer for half an hour to make slicing easier, if desired.

1. Heat the oil in a heavy, large skillet or wok. Add the beef and frozen snow peas.
2. Stir-fry until the beef is browned and the peas are tender crisp.
3. Mix the remaining ingredients thoroughly.
4. Add the sauce to the beef and snow peas, stirring constantly. When the mixture comes to a boil, simmer for 1 minute. Serve immediately.

Meat Loaf

6–8 SERVINGS

1½ pounds lean ground beef
2 eggs
½ cup quick-cooking oatmeal
1 medium-size onion, diced
2 tablespoons prepared mustard
1 tablespoon Worcestershire sauce
salt and pepper to taste
¼ cup milk

1. Preheat the oven to 375°F.
2. Place the beef in a large bowl.
3. Measure the remaining ingredients into a blender container and blend until smooth.
4. Pour over the beef and mix thoroughly.
5. Turn the mixture into an 8½x4x2½-inch meat loaf pan sprayed with vegetable oil.
6. Bake in the preheated oven for 1¼–1½ hours. Let stand for 10 minutes before serving.

Variations:

To bake this meat loaf in a slow-cooker, omit the milk. Place a piece of foil on a baking rack in the cooker and punch a few holes in the foil with a fork so the fat can drain. Place the shaped meat loaf on the foil-lined rack, put the cover in place, and cook on low for 8–10 hours.

You can bake mini meat loaves in muffin tins filled just level with the top of the tin. This recipe makes 12. Bake in a 375°F. oven for 20–25 minutes. To freeze, remove from the tins and freeze on cookie sheets; then package loosely in food-safe plastic bags. To reheat, place the frozen meat loaves on a cookie sheet, bake for 15–20 minutes at 375°F. (just until heated through) or reheat in a microwave oven for 3–4 minutes per serving.

Slow-Cooker Roast Pork

9–12 SERVINGS

1 4–5-pound boneless pork roast
2 tablespoons vegetable oil
salt and pepper
garlic powder

This roast is finished in a conventional oven.

1. Trim the roast of all excess fat. Then heat the oil in a heavy skillet and brown the roast on all sides.
2. Place the roast on a rack in a slow-cooker. Sprinkle it with the seasonings.
3. Cover the top of the cooker with 4 layers of paper towel. Put the cover snugly in place. Set the cooker on low (200°F.) and cook for 8–10 hours.
4. Preheat the oven to 325°F.
5. Transfer the roast to a roasting pan and insert a meat thermometer.
6. Finish roasting the meat in a conventional oven set at 325°F. for 45–60 minutes or until the meat thermometer registers 170°F. Serve.

Pork Cutlet Parmesan

This is a good recipe for using leftover roast pork. Heat the oil over a hot heat — it will not spatter unless you put food or water in it. Cooking food can be covered with a spatter screen (available in hardware stores) to prevent burns. If you do not have a temperature-controlled electric frying pan, test the temperature of the oil with a deep-fat thermometer.

4 SERVINGS

vegetable oil
1 egg
1 tablespoon milk
¾ cup breadcrumbs (or more as needed)
¾ cup grated Parmesan cheese
¼ teaspoon salt
dash pepper
¼ teaspoon dried basil
1 teaspoon dried parsley
⅛ teaspoon garlic powder
8 ¼-inch-thick slices leftover roast pork
1 cup tomato sauce
4 ounces grated mozzarella cheese

1. Preheat the oven to 400°F.
2. Fill a large skillet with vegetable oil to a depth of 1 inch.
3. Beat the milk into the egg in a shallow bowl.
4. Mix the breadcrumbs, Parmesan cheese, and seasonings.
5. Dip the pork slices in the egg mixture, then in the seasoned crumbs to coat.
6. Fry the pork in the hot (385°F.) oil until it is brown on both sides. Drain on paper towels.
7. Place the drained pork slices in a baking dish sprayed with vegetable oil.
8. Top with the tomato sauce and cheese.
9. Bake in the preheated oven until the cheese melts, approximately 10 minutes. Serve.

Baked Ham with Pineapple

4 SERVINGS

¼ cup brown sugar
¼ teaspoon ground cloves
1 2–3-pound canned ham
1 8-ounce can chunk pineapple, drained

This dish can be cooked with other casserole dishes in ovens up to 375°F. Reserve the pineapple juice to serve as a beverage.

1. Preheat the oven to 325°F.
2. Mix the sugar and cloves and spread the mixture over the ham.
3. Place the pineapple chunks on top of the ham. Hold them in place with toothpicks.
4. Bake in the preheated oven for 1 hour at 325°F. or 45 minutes at 375°F. Serve.

Lamb Stew

4–6 SERVINGS

2 large potatoes, peeled and cut in 1-inch chunks
1 pound frozen tiny whole onions
1 pound frozen sliced carrots
1 cup hot water
1 can cream of chicken soup
¼ cup grape jelly
½ teaspoon dried rosemary
2 pounds lean stewing lamb, cut in 2-inch chunks

For a thicker broth, omit the vegetable water and thicken the stew with flour or dehydrated potato buds.

1. Put the potatoes, frozen onions, and frozen carrots in a large saucepan (with the potatoes on the bottom). Add 1 cup of hot tap water. Cover the pan and bring the vegetables to a boil.

2. Cook the vegetables for 5 minutes. Drain, reserving ¼ cup of the vegetable water.

3. While the vegetables are cooking, measure the chicken soup, grape jelly, and rosemary into a blender. Add ¼ cup of the reserved vegetable water to the blender and blend until smooth.

4. Put the vegetables into the bottom of a slow-cooker. Top with the lamb pieces. Pour the blender contents over all. Cover and cook on low (200°F.) for 8–10 hours.

CHAPTER 8
SALADS and DRESSINGS

24-Hour Salad

4 SERVINGS

1½ cups torn lettuce
1½ cups torn fresh spinach
1 large sweet onion, sliced, separated into rings
1 cup frozen peas
½ cup mayonnaise
¼ cup sour cream
1 tablespoon milk-and-mayonnaise-type buttermilk dressing mix powder

This salad should be made at least 12 hours before serving. Do not defrost the peas before adding them to the salad.

1. Layer the lettuce, spinach, onion rings, and *frozen* peas in a medium-size bowl.
2. Mix the mayonnaise, sour cream, and dressing mix powder. Pour over the salad. Cover the salad completely with the dressing — do not mix it in.
3. Cover the bowl tightly and refrigerate overnight.
4. To serve, mix the dressing with the salad vegetables.

Variation:
Add ¼ pound diced, crisp, cooked bacon.

Frozen Fruit Salad

This is a good salad to keep in the freezer for unexpected guests.

If you are not going to use the entire salad, refreeze the unused portion immediately.

8 SERVINGS

- 1 3-ounce package lemon- or orange-flavored gelatin
- dash salt
- 1 cup boiling water
- 1 8¾-ounce can pineapple tidbits
- ¼ cup lemon juice
- ⅓ cup mayonnaise
- 1 cup whipping cream, or 2 cups frozen whipped topping, defrosted
- 1 medium-size banana, diced
- ½ cup seeded grapes, cut in halves
- ¼ cup maraschino cherries, cut in halves
- ¼ cup chopped nuts

1. Dissolve the gelatin and salt in the boiling water.
2. Drain the pineapple. Reserve the juice. Add water to the juice to make ½ cup.
3. Add the juice to the dissolved gelatin with the lemon juice.
4. Blend in the mayonnaise.
5. Chill until very thick. It should mound on a spoon but not be completely jelled.
6. Whip the cream until thick (or use whipped topping).
7. Fold into the gelatin mixture.
8. Fold in the fruit and nuts.
9. Pour into a 9x5x3-inch loaf pan sprayed with vegetable oil, and freeze.
10. To serve, turn the pan upside down under running cold water for a minute or two. Loosen the edges of the salad. Unmold onto a serving dish. Slice into 8 equal servings.

Cabbage, Carrot, and Raisin Salad

4 SERVINGS

2 cups shredded cabbage
½ cup shredded carrot
¼ cup raisins
¼ teaspoon celery seed
2 tablespoons vegetable oil
2 teaspoons vinegar
1 teaspoon honey
salt and pepper to taste

1. Combine all the ingredients.
2. Chill until serving time.

Buttermilk Dressing

1½ CUPS

1 cup mayonnaise
6 tablespoons buttermilk
⅓ teaspoon onion powder
⅓ teaspoon garlic powder
1 teaspoon dried parsley
1 teaspoon dried chives
⅛ teaspoon dry mustard
1 tablespoon lemon juice
dash salt

1. Blend all the ingredients thoroughly in a blender or with a wire whisk.
2. Refrigerate for several hours to blend the flavors.

Creamy Italian Dressing

1½ CUPS

1 cup mayonnaise
6 tablespoons milk
1½ teaspoons Italian seasoning
½ teaspoon garlic powder
½ teaspoon onion powder

1. Blend all the ingredients thoroughly in a blender or with a wire whisk.
2. Refrigerate for several hours to blend the flavors.

Blue Cheese Dressing

2 CUPS

3½ ounces blue cheese
1 cup mayonnaise
½ cup light cream
2 teaspoons honey
1 teaspoon lemon juice
dash hot pepper sauce
dash garlic powder
¼ teaspoon dried parsley

1. Divide the blue cheese in half. Put half in a blender container with the remaining ingredients and blend until smooth.
2. Pour the blender contents into a 2-cup covered container.
3. Crumble the remaining blue cheese over the dressing and stir it in.
4. Refrigerate for several hours to blend the flavors.

Thousand Island Dressing

1¼ CUPS

1 hard-boiled egg
½ cup mayonnaise
½ cup sweet pickle relish, drained

1. Chop the egg very fine.
2. Add the remaining ingredients and mix well.
3. Refrigerate for 1 hour before serving, to blend the flavors.

Oil and Vinegar Dressing

1 PINT

1½ cups vegetable oil
½ cup cider vinegar
2 small garlic cloves, minced fine
2 teaspoons honey
¼ teaspoon salt (optional)
⅛ teaspoon pepper
½ teaspoon paprika
1 teaspoon dry mustard

If you want a tangier dressing, use slightly more vinegar. This dressing does not need to be refrigerated.

1. Measure all the ingredients into a 2-cup jar.
2. Shake well to blend, and shake well before using.

Tomato Soup French Dressing

4½–5 CUPS

- 2 tablespoons dry mustard
- 2 teaspoon salt
- 6 tablespoons honey
- 2 cups vegetable oil
- 2 tablespoons chopped onion
- 1 cup cider vinegar
- 1 can tomato soup

1. Measure all the ingredients into a blender container and blend until smooth.
2. Refrigerate to blend the flavors.

CHAPTER 9
SAUCES and DIPS

All of these sauces and dressings can be made up ahead of time for the recipes in this and the following sections. Chopping, slicing and shredding extra vegetables ahead of time for salads, quiches, omelets and casseroles, will keep actual meal preparation time down to a matter of minutes.

Instant Sweet and Sour Sauce

Use this sauce as a baste for meat and poultry, a sauce for egg rolls, or a dip for fried chicken or fish nuggets.

1½ CUPS

½ cup ketchup
½ cup unsweetened apple-sauce
½ cup peach preserves
2 generous dashes cayenne
dash salt
¼ teaspoon garlic powder
1 teaspoon onion powder

1. Measure everything into a blender container and blend until smooth.
2. Heat in a small saucepan to blend the flavors.
3. Cool and refrigerate in a covered container.

Super-Quick Cheese Sauce

This sauce can be served over vegetables. It also makes a delicious baked macaroni and cheese or cheesy scalloped potatoes.

1¾ CUPS

1 can cream of celery soup
4 ounces cheddar or Velveeta® cheese, cubed

1. Blend the soup and cheese in a blender until smooth.
2. Pour into a small saucepan and heat until the cheese has melted. Stir constantly.

South-of-the-Border Salsa

Very hot!!!
Serve with tacos, scrambled eggs, **Mexicali Omelet** (p. 108), huevos rancheros, or as a condiment with meat and fish.

4 CUPS

4 cups canned tomatoes with juices
½ cup chopped fresh cilantro leaves, or 1½ tablespoons dried cilantro
1 large onion, diced
1 small fresh or canned jalapeño pepper, seeds and all, minced fine
¼ teaspoon garlic powder
salt and pepper to taste

1. Put all the ingredients in a small saucepan and simmer for 20 minutes.
2. Cool and refrigerate in a covered container.

Sauce for Stir-Fried Dishes

Keep one jar of this sauce made up with chicken broth and one made up with beef broth in the refrigerator all the time. Stir-fry leftover meat, poultry, or fish with some vegetables and thicken with a little of this sauce for an almost instant Chinese dinner; 1 cup is enough for four servings of meat and vegetables.

Canned broths work well in this recipe, and they keep indefinitely. Sauce made with homemade broth will keep for about 10 days in the refrigerator.

2 CUPS

- 2 cups *Homemade Beef Stock,* p. 86, *Rich Chicken Broth,* p. 85, or canned broth
- 3 tablespoons soy sauce
- 2 tablespoons plus 1 teaspoon cornstarch
- 1 generous dish cayenne or Chinese hot oil
- ⅛ teaspoon garlic powder
- 2 teaspoons brown sugar

1. Measure all the ingredients into a jar and shake well to mix.
2. Store in the refrigerator to be used as needed.

Never-Fail Gravy

The most frequent problem that inexperienced cooks have with making gravy is determining how much water to add to pan juices. It's pretty safe to start with 1 cup for a small roast (3-4 pounds) and 2 cups for a large roast (10 pounds). Use broth if you have it — it will stretch the gravy considerably. Always use cold water or cold broth. Extend juices from poultry, pork, and veal with chicken broth, from beef and older veal with beef broth.

pan juices
salt and pepper to taste
all-purpose flour
beef or chicken broth

1. Bring the juices to a boil, stirring and scraping to loosen the small bits of browned meat from the bottom of the pan.
2. Season lightly with salt and pepper and taste the juices. If they are very rich tasting, add more water or broth, a little at a time, tasting as you go along.
3. When you feel that you have stretched the pan juices as much as you can while retaining good flavor, remove the pan from the heat and pour the juices into a blender container. Do not fill the blender more than half full.
4. Let the juices stand for a minute or two to allow the fat to rise to the surface. If there is too much fat (more than 2 tablespoons per cup of juice), skim the excess fat from the juices.
5. Add 1½-2 tablespoons flour (1½ for thin gravy, 2 for thick) to the blender for each cup of juice and blend until smooth.
6. Return the juices to the pan. Cook over medium heat, stirring constantly, until the gravy has thickened. Continue to heat for 2 minutes to cook the flour. Adjust seasonings.

Quick-and-Easy Pasta Sauce

Reduce the amount of red pepper if you prefer a milder sauce. This simple sauce tastes as if it had been simmered for hours, yet it can be ready in less than 20 minutes.

4 SERVINGS

1 pound lean ground beef
½ cup diced onion
6 ounces tomato paste
1½ cups water
1½ teaspoons dried basil
¼ teaspoon garlic powder
⅛ teaspoon crushed red pepper
salt and pepper to taste

1. Sauté the beef in a large, heavy skillet sprayed with vegetable oil.
2. Add the remaining ingredients and stir well to mix.
3. Bring to a boil; then reduce the heat and cook, uncovered, for 10 minutes.
4. Serve over any kind of pasta.

Spaghetti Sauce for Meatballs

Frozen meatballs do not have to be thawed before being added to this sauce — they will thaw while the sauce is simmering.

1 QUART

12 ounces tomato paste
3 cups water
1 tablespoon dried basil
¼ teaspoon garlic powder
⅛ teaspoon crushed red pepper
1 tablespoon dried parsley
2 teaspoons salt
pepper to taste
30 meatballs, p. 137 (optional)

1. Measure all the ingredients except the meatballs into a 3-quart saucepan and stir to mix.
2. Add the meatballs.
3. Bring the sauce to a boil. Then reduce the heat and simmer for 15–20 minutes.
4. Serve over cooked spaghetti or noodles.

Herb Dip

2 CUPS

1 pound ricotta cheese
¼ cup light cream or milk
1 package herb-seasoned salad dressing mix powder
generous dash garlic powder

Any flavor salad dressing mix powder can be used in this recipe; however, I think the country style dressing that calls for mayonnaise and milk works best.

1. Put all the ingredients in a food processor bowl fitted with a steel chopping blade and process until smooth.
2. Refrigerate for at least ½ hour to blend the flavors.

Cocktail Sauce for Meatballs

SAUCE FOR 50 MEATBALLS

12 ounces seafood cocktail sauce
½ cup grape jelly
1 tablespoon instant coffee granules (regular or decaf)

Simple, crazy, but surprisingly good. Frozen meatballs do not have to be thawed before being added to this sauce.

1. Combine all the ingredients and heat until the jelly and the coffee granules have dissolved.
2. Add the meatballs and continue heating in a covered pan over very low heat until the meatballs are heated through. Serve warm.

CHAPTER 10
DESSERTS

Most of the desserts in this chapter are based on homemade quick mixes. Never be without them if you want to save hours of food-preparation time.

Molded salads can be made up ahead of time and kept refrigerated for several days. The molded Orange Pineapple Cream salad keeps refrigerated for weeks when made with commercially prepared frozen whipped topping. Molded salads made with sweetened whipped cream, however, have a shelf life of just 2–3 days at most. After that they begin to get watery.

Fudge Brownies

20 BROWNIES

2½ cups *Chocolate Cake Mix,* p. 63, stirred well before measuring
1 teaspoon vanilla
1 tablespoon cider vinegar
¾ cup cold water
9 tablespoons vegetable oil
½ cup chopped walnuts

1. Preheat the oven to 350°F.
2. Measure the cake mix into a small bowl.
3. Mix the vanilla and vinegar and set aside.
4. Mix the water and oil and set aside.
5. Poke 3 evenly spaced holes in the dry mix. Pour equal amounts of the vinegar mixture into these holes.
6. Pour the water-oil mixture over all. *Fold* the water mixture into the dry mix with a wire whisk. Do not beat. Stir in nuts.
7. Pour the batter into a lightly greased and floured 9x13-inch Pyrex baking dish. Bake in preheated oven for 20 minutes.
8. Cool on a wire rack. Cut into twenty pieces, and serve.

Quick-and-Easy Chocolate Cake

It is very important that the oven be preheated before you mix this cake. The cake should be mixed and immediately put into a fully preheated oven. This recipe makes a single layer — see the Variation to make a double-layer cake.

8 SERVINGS

2½ cups *Chocolate Cake Mix,* p. 63, stirred well before measuring
1 teaspoon vanilla
1 tablespoon cider vinegar
1 cup cold water
6 tablespoons vegetable oil

1. Preheat the oven to 350°F.
2. Measure the cake mix into a small bowl.
3. Mix the vanilla and vinegar and set aside.
4. Mix the water and oil and set aside.
5. Poke 3 evenly spaced holes in the dry mix. Pour equal amounts of the vinegar mixture into these holes.
6. Pour the water-oil mixture over all. *Fold* the water-oil mixture into the dry mix with a wire whisk. Do not beat or the cake will not rise.
7. Pour the batter into a lightly greased and floured 8-inch round or square Pyrex baking dish.
8. Bake in the preheated oven for 35–45 minutes or until a toothpick inserted in the center comes out clean.
9. Cool on a wire rack.
10. Frost with your favorite frosting or *Quick-and-Easy Chocolate Frosting* (p. 161), or serve warm with whipped cream.

Variation:
 To make a double-layer cake, use 3¾ cups **Chocolate Cake Mix,** 1½ teaspoons vanilla, 1½ tablespoons cider vinegar, 1½ cups cold water, and 9 tablespoons vegetable oil. Assemble as directed. Divide the batter into two 8-inch, lightly greased and floured pans. Bake for 30–35 minutes. Frost as directed.

Quick-and-Easy Chocolate Frosting

FROSTS ONE DOUBLE-LAYER CAKE

13 ounces sweetened condensed milk
2 ounces unsweetened chocolate
2-4 tablespoons water
dash salt
1 teaspoon vanilla

1. Place all of the ingredients in a small, heavy saucepan. Use only 2 tablespoons of water at first.

2. Cook over medium heat, stirring constantly, until the chocolate has melted and the frosting has thickened. If the frosting becomes too thick, gradually add small amounts of water until it is the desired consistency.

Variation: Hot Fudge Sauce
 Thin the frosting with water to the desired consistency and substitute rum extract for the vanilla. Serve over ice cream or pound cake.

Chocolate Cream Roll

This lovely dessert is best if frozen for about an hour or refrigerated for several hours before serving. You can impress unexpected guests with **Chocolate Cream Roll** for an elegant finish to an impromptu dinner. These easy-to-make rolls can be frosted while still frozen and will defrost in about an hour at room temperature. Keep several on hand in the freezer.

For an even quicker way to serve these, make up rolls as directed; then frost and freeze until slightly firm and easy to slice. Slice in individual-serving-size pieces, tray-freeze, overwrap when frozen, and place in plastic bags or a sturdy container. These slices will defrost in 10–15 minutes at room temperature.

8–10 SERVINGS

4 egg whites
1 recipe *Quick and Easy Chocolate Cake batter*, p. 160
8 ounces sweetened whipped cream or 1 8-ounce package frozen whipped topping, defrosted
1 package rum-flavored Life Savers
1 recipe *Quick and Easy Chocolate Frosting*, p. 161
½ cup finely chopped walnuts

1. Preheat the oven to 350°F.
2. Beat the egg whites until stiff but not dry.
3. Fold the cake batter into the egg whites carefully with a wire whisk.
4. Pour the mixture into a lightly greased and floured 12x18-inch jellyroll pan.
5. Bake in the preheated oven for 15 minutes or until the top springs back.
6. Remove the cake from the oven and cover it with a large, damp towel. Leave one end of the towel longer than the other. Put another pan of the same size (or a large piece of stiff cardboard) on top of the cake. The bottom of the pan should be on top of the cake, on the towel.

7. Turn the two pans upside down. Lift the baking pan off the cake. Slip the other pan from under the towel.

8. Roll the extended end of the towel first (to form a core for your cake); then continue rolling the cake up in the towel. Place the rolled cake on a wire rack to cool for about 45 minutes.

9. Unroll the cooled cake (leave the towel under it).

10. Frost with whipped topping. Cover the cake evenly, but don't go too close to the edge.

11. Put the Life Savers in a plastic bag and crush them with a hammer. Then sprinkle them over the whipped topping.

12. Reroll the cake. When you get to the end, lift the towel and roll the cake onto a serving plate, or onto heavy-duty foil if you are going to freeze it. Freeze without frosting.

13. Frost the cake with the chocolate frosting and sprinkle with chopped nuts.

14. Refrigerate until serving time.

Brownie Hot Fudge Sundae

4 SERVINGS

2-3 cups vanilla ice cream
4 large brownies
Hot Fudge Sauce, **p. 161**
chopped nuts

1. Place a scoop of ice cream on top of each brownie.
2. Pour fudge sauce over the ice cream.
3. Sprinkle chopped nuts over all.
4. Serve.

5-Minute Fudge

When I say it takes 5 minutes to make this fudge, I mean from the time you start to take everything out of the cupboard until you finish the fudge and put everything away. Try it for yourself! This fudge is best stored in a cool area — not necessarily the refrigerator.

1½ POUNDS

14 ounces sweetened condensed milk
12 ounces semi-sweet chocolate bits
1 teaspoon vanilla
dash salt
⅓ cup chopped walnuts

1. Place all the ingredients, except the nuts, in a 1½-quart heavy saucepan.

2. Cook over medium-hot heat, stirring constantly, until the chocolate bits have melted and the mixture is smooth. Stir in nuts.

3. Scrape the mixture into an 8-inch square baking dish that has been sprayed with vegetable oil. Sprinkle the nuts over the top.

4. Cool at room temperature for a few minutes. Then refrigerate to finish setting. Cut into 1-inch squares.

Variations:

To make peanut butter fudge, substitute peanut-butter-flavored bits for the chocolate bits and add ¼ cup peanut butter to the batter. You can also substitute peanuts for the walnuts if you wish.

To make butterscotch fudge, substitute butterscotch-flavored bits for the chocolate bits.

Strawberry Pie

8 SERVINGS

- 1 pint fresh strawberries, or 2 cups frozen unsweetened berries (do not defrost)
- 1 6-ounce package strawberry-flavored gelatin
- 1 cup boiling water
- 1 cup crushed ice or ice cubes
- 1 cup ricotta cheese
- 1 cup frozen whipped topping, defrosted
- 1 graham cracker pie crust (homemade or packaged)

1. Wash, hull, and slice fresh berries or slice frozen berries (keep them frozen).
2. Place the gelatin in a blender container.
3. Add 1 cup boiling water and blend to dissolve the gelatin.
4. Add 1 cup ricotta cheese to the blender container.
5. Measure crushed ice or ice cubes into a 1-cup measure. Add cold water to the 1 cup line. Pour the ice and water into the blender and blend until smooth. Pour into a medium-size bowl.
6. Fold in the whipped topping and the strawberries. Pour the mixture into the prepared pie crust.
7. Refrigerate, covered with plastic wrap, until serving time.

Magic Crust Pumpkin Pie

8 SERVINGS

16 ounces canned pumpkin
14 ounces evaporated milk
2 tablespoons butter or margarine, softened
2 eggs
¾ cup sugar
½ cup *Baking Powder Biscuit Mix,* p. 68, stirred well before measuring
2½ teaspoons pumpkin pie spice
2 teaspoons vanilla

1. Preheat the oven to 350°F.
2. Measure all the ingredients into a blender container and blend until smooth.
3. Pour the blender contents into a 10x1½-inch, deep-dish pie plate sprayed with vegetable oil.
4. Bake in the preheated oven for 50–55 minutes or until a knife inserted in the center comes out clean.
5. Cool on a wire rack. Serve.

Magic Crust Cheesecake

8 SERVINGS

¾ cup milk
2 teaspoons vanilla
2 eggs
1 cup sugar
½ cup *Baking Powder Biscuit Mix,* p. 68, stirred well before measuring
16 ounces cream cheese, cut in cubes
1 tablespoon lemon juice
fruit preserves

1. Preheat the oven to 350°F.
2. Measure all the ingredients (except the fruit preserves) into a blender container and blend until smooth.
3. Pour the mixture into a 10x1½-inch, deep-dish pie plate sprayed with vegetable oil.
4. Bake in the preheated oven for 40–45 minutes or until a knife inserted near the center comes out clean.
5. Cool to room temperature on a wire rack and then refrigerate until chilled (at least 2 hours).

6. Mix your favorite preserves (mine is raspberry jam) with a little water, just enough to thin the preserves slightly. Spread over the cheesecake before serving.

Magic Crust Chocolate Fudge Pie

This pie is especially good served warm with whipped cream or ice cream.

8 SERVINGS

4 eggs
½ **cup brown sugar, packed**
½ **cup** *Baking Powder Biscuit Mix,* **p. 68, stirred well before measuring**
½ **cup granulated sugar**
¼ **cup butter or margarine**
⅔ **cup semi-sweet chocolate bits (4 ounces)**
¾ **cup chopped walnuts**

1. Preheat the oven to 350°F.
2. Put the eggs, brown sugar, biscuit mix, and granulated sugar in a blender container and blend until smooth.
3. Melt the butter and the chocolate bits in a small, heavy saucepan. Cool slightly.
4. With the blender running, pour the melted chocolate into the blender container, scraping out the saucepan with a rubber spatula. Blend thoroughly.
5. Pour the blender contents into a 9-inch Pyrex pie plate sprayed with vegetable oil.
6. Sprinkle the nuts over the top.
7. Bake in the preheated oven for 30–35 minutes or until a knife inserted in the center comes out clean.
8. Cool on a wire rack. Serve warm or cold.

Magic Crust Maple Walnut Pie

8 SERVINGS

¾ cup milk
¾ cup maple syrup
¼ cup butter or margarine, softened
2 teaspoons maple flavoring or vanilla extract
4 eggs
¾ cup brown sugar, packed
¾ cup *Baking Powder Biscuit Mix,* p. 68, stirred well before measuring
1½ cups chopped walnuts

1. Preheat the oven to 350°F.
2. Measure all the ingredients, except the walnuts, into a blender container and blend until smooth.
3. Spread the walnuts in a 9-inch Pyrex pie plate sprayed with vegetable oil.
4. Pour the blender contents over the walnuts.
5. Bake in the preheated oven for 40–45 minutes or until a knife inserted in the center comes out clean.

Variation:
   Substitute chopped pecans for the walnuts and dark corn syrup for the maple syrup.

Rich Peach Shortcake

4 SERVINGS

- 1 cup *Baking Powder Biscuit Mix*, p. 68, stirred well before measuring
- 1 tablespoon sugar
- ⅓ cup all-purpose whipping cream, or more to make a moist but stiff dough
- 1 16-ounce can sliced peaches
- 1 cup frozen whipped topping, defrosted

This shortcake can be served with any fresh or canned fruit.

1. Preheat the oven to 450°F.
2. Measure the biscuit mix into a bowl.
3. Stir in the sugar.
4. Stir in the cream. The dough should be moist, but the batter should hold its shape.
5. Drop the batter by tablespoons onto an ungreased cookie sheet.
6. Bake in the preheated oven for 12–15 minutes or until nicely browned on top.
7. Split the biscuits and top with the sliced peaches and ¼ cup whipped topping per serving.

Peanut Butter Cookies

40 COOKIES

14 ounces sweetened condensed milk
1½ teaspoons vanilla
½ cup peanut butter, smooth or chunky
2 cups *Baking Powder Biscuit Mix*, p. 68, stirred well before measuring
sugar

If anyone finds a faster cookie to make, I wish they would write and let me know.

1. Preheat the oven to 350°F.
2. Mix all the ingredients with an electric mixer until well blended.
3. Drop the batter by teaspoons onto a cookie sheet sprayed with vegetable oil. Leave 4 inches between cookies.
4. Dip a flat-bottomed glass in sugar and use it to press the cookies flat.
5. Bake in the preheated oven for 9–10 minutes or until the cookies are lightly browned around the edges. Cool on wire racks.

Instant Rice Pudding

4 SERVINGS

1½ cups milk
1½ tablespoons butter or margarine
¼ teaspoon cinnamon
⅛ teaspoon nutmeg
¼ cup honey or sugar
1 teaspoon vanilla
½ cup raisins
1½ cups instant rice, uncooked
½ cup light cream

1. Measure the milk, butter, cinnamon, nutmeg, honey, vanilla, and raisins into a 1-quart saucepan.
2. Bring the mixture to a boil. Stir in the rice. Cover the pan and remove from the heat.
3. Let stand for 8 minutes.
4. Stir in the cream.
5. Serve warm or cold with a whipped topping.

Chocolate Chip Cookies

4 DOZEN COOKIES

14 ounces sweetened condensed milk
1½ teaspoons vanilla or maple flavoring
⅓ cup vegetable shortening
1 egg
2½ cups *Baking Powder Biscuit* Mix, p. 68, stirred well before measuring
1 cup chocolate bits
½ cup chopped nuts

1. Preheat the oven to 375°F.
2. Blend the milk, vanilla, shortening, and egg with ½ cup of the biscuit mix until smooth. Blend in the remaining biscuit mix.
3. Stir in the chocolate bits and nuts.
4. Drop the batter by teaspoons onto a cookie sheet sprayed with vegetable oil. Leave 3 inches between cookies.
5. Bake in the preheated oven for 10 minutes. The cookies will not get dark brown. Cool on wire racks.

Crisp Sugar Cookies

30 LARGE COOKIES

14 ounces sweetened condensed milk
1½ teaspoons lemon extract
3 cups *Baking Powder Biscuit* Mix, p. 68, stirred well before measuring
sugar

1. Preheat the oven to 375°F.
2. Stir all the ingredients together until well blended.
3. Drop the batter by rounded tablespoons onto a cookie sheet sprayed with vegetable oil.
4. Dip a flat-bottomed glass in sugar and use it to press the cookies thin.
5. Bake in the preheated oven for 8–10 minutes or until the cookies are slightly browned around the edges.
6. Remove the cookies from the cookie sheet and cool on wire racks.

Fruit Crisp

6–8 SERVINGS

2 tablespoons butter, softened
½ cup brown sugar
4 cups fresh, frozen, or canned, drained fruit
1⅓ cups *Fruit Crisp Topping* (p. 65)

1. Preheat the oven to 350°F.
2. Grease an 8-inch Pyrex baking dish with the softened butter. Use all of it.
3. Sprinkle the brown sugar over the bottom of the dish.
4. Put the fruit in the dish.
5. Top with the *Fruit Crisp Topping.*
6. Bake until the top is browned and the fruit is cooked, about 40 minutes.
7. Serve warm with a whipped topping.

Molded Orange Pineapple Cream

The most effective way to drain pineapple for molded salads is to place the pineapple in a fine sieve, place the sieve over a deep bowl, top the pineapple with a saucer, and then top the saucer with a quart jar of water. Pineapple drained this way will have a minimum of moisture and will make a nice firm molded salad.

This dessert takes about 3 hours to set completely, but it soft-sets in about 30 minutes.

6–8 SERVINGS

- 1 6-ounce package orange-flavored gelatin
- ½ cup boiling water
- 2 cups ice cubes
- 1 cup well-drained crushed pineapple, juice reserved
- 1½ cups ricotta cheese
- 1 cup sweetened whipped cream or 1 cup frozen whipped topping, defrosted

1. Put the gelatin in a 2-cup Pyrex measuring cup. Pour the boiling water over the gelatin and stir to dissolve.
2. Put this mixture into a blender container.
3. Measure 2 cups of ice cubes. Add pineapple juice and water to bring the liquid up to the 2-cup line.
4. Add the ice to the blender with the ricotta cheese. Blend until very smooth. The mixture will start to thicken.
5. Pour the mixture into a medium-size bowl. Fold in the pineapple and whipped topping.
6. Pour into a 6-cup mold sprayed with vegetable oil and chill until set, about 3 hours.

Fruited Mousse

6–8 SERVINGS

1 6-ounce package flavored gelatin
1 cup boiling water
1 cup ice cubes or crushed ice
1 cup ricotta or cottage cheese
¼ cup sugar

When using strawberry or raspberry gelatin, add 1 teaspoon of lemon juice to the mixture. This will pick up the flavor considerably. Empty margarine tubs or frozen whipped topping containers make good molds.

1. Place the flavored gelatin in a blender container. Add the boiling water and blend to dissolve the gelatin.

2. Fill a 1-cup measuring cup with ice cubes or crushed ice. Add cold water to the 1-cup line. Add the ice and water to the blender container.

3. Measure the cheese into the blender container and add the sugar. Blend until smooth.

4. Pour into a 4-cup refrigerator container or mold and chill until set (15–20 minutes).

APPENDICES

Suggested Substitutions

If your recipe calls for:	You may substitute:
1 cup beef or chicken broth	1 cup water with 2 teaspoons *powdered* beef or chicken bouillon; reduce salt in the recipe by 1 teaspoon
butter	margarine
butter, margarine, or oil	meat drippings (pork, beef, bacon, chicken, ham, or turkey); especially good in gravies and stir-fried dishes
1 cup cake flour	⅞ cup all-purpose flour with 2 tablespoons cornstarch
1 ounce semi-sweet chocolate	1 ounce chocolate bits
1 ounce unsweetened chocolate	3 tablespoons unsweetened cocoa plus 1 tablespoon butter or shortening
1 cup cream	1 cup whole milk with ⅓ cup powdered dry milk and 1 tablespoon butter 1 cup double-strength reconstituted dry milk with 2 tablespoons butter 1 cup evaporated milk
8 ounces cream cheese	8 ounces well-drained ricotta cheese
1 egg	2 egg yolks or 2 egg whites plus 1 teaspoon vegetable oil
1 cup fish stock	1 cup bottled clam juice

If your recipe calls for:	You may substitute:
1 tablespoon flour for thickening	½ tablespoon cornstarch (Use this for recipes that will not require reheating since cornstarch breaks down quickly when reheated.) 2 tablespoons quick-cooking tapioca 1 tablespoon granular tapioca 2 tablespoons granular cereal
1 tablespoon fresh chopped herbs	1 teaspoon dried herbs
shrimp, crab, or lobster	Canned shrimp, crab, lobster, or the new look-alike products that are a preformed combination of seafood such as crabmeat and pollock
1 can condensed soup	1½ cups thick homemade cream soup of a similar type
1 cup sour cream	1 cup yogurt 1 cup non-butterfat sour cream substitute
1 cup sour milk or buttermilk	Scant 1 cup whole milk with 1 tablespoon lemon juice or vinegar 1 cup water mixed with 4 tablespoons Saco dry buttermilk powder (available in the baking section of the supermarket)
1 cup of sugar	¾ cup honey with a pinch of baking soda 1 cup firmly packed brown sugar 1 cup molasses plus ½ teaspoon baking soda; omit ¼ cup liquid from the recipe 1½ cups maple syrup; omit ½ cup liquid from the recipe

If your recipe calls for:	You may substitute:
1 cup tomato sauce	1 cup canned tomato sauce
	2 cups tomato juice; cook until reduced by half
	4 ounces tomato paste plus 4 ounces water with 1 teaspoon sugar and ½ teaspoon dried basil
1 cup white sauce	1 cup cream of chicken or cream of celery soup

PANTRY STAPLES

- Vegetable oil (preferably corn oil)
- Solid vegetable shortening
- White sugar
- Brown sugar
- Honey
- Molasses
- All-purpose unbleached flour
- Whole wheat flour
- Cornstarch
- Baking powder
- Baking soda
- Vanilla
- Pepper
- Salt
- Basil
- Oregano
- Bay leaves
- Italian seasoning
- Dry mustard
- Garlic powder
- Onion powder
- Dry celery flakes
- Dry parsley flakes
- Cinnamon
- Nutmeg
- Cloves, powdered and whole
- Ground allspice
- Crushed red pepper
- Poultry seasoning
- Ground sage
- Mace
- Sweet marjoram
- Thyme
- Paprika
- Cream of tartar
- Worcestershire sauce
- Hot pepper sauce
- Ketchup
- Prepared mustard (2-3 kinds)
- Potatoes
- Onions, fresh and dehydrated
- Milk, fresh and powdered
- Butter or margarine
- Eggs
- Powdered beef bouillon
- Powdered chicken bouillon
- Mace
- Unsweetened cocoa
- Chocolate bits
- Bottled clam juice
- Canned chicken and beef broth
- Creamed soups (chicken, celery, mushroom, and shrimp)
- Instant and regular white or brown rice

Glossary

Au jus	Natural unthickened meat broth.
Baste	To spoon a flavored broth or sauce over food during cooking.
Blanch	To pour boiling water over food; or to place food in water, bring to a boil, and drain. In some cases the food (such as tomatoes, peaches, or almonds) is then covered with cold water to facilitate peeling.
Cream	To beat until smooth, light, and fluffy.
Crush	To press to extract juice, usually used when speaking of garlic; the side of a knife or a garlic press can be used.
Cut in	To distribute solid fats in dry ingredients by slicing through the mixture repeatedly with knives, a pastry blender, or a food processor fitted with a chopping blade.
Deglaze	To loosen bits of browned meat from the cooking pan by adding broth or water and stirring over medium-high heat.
Dice	To cut in cubes about the size of the end of your little finger.
Fold	To combine ingredients lightly by the use of a downward vertical motion through the mixture, across the bottom of the bowl, and back up the side — in effect turning the mixture over while incorporating ingredients at the same time.
Glaze	To coat with sugar syrup or melted jelly or preserves either during or after cooking.
Julienne	To cut into matchlike sticks.
Marinate	To let food soak in liquid that will tenderize and add flavor to it.
Mince	To chop very fine.

Parboil	To simmer in liquid a short time before cooking by some other method.
Pare	To cut off the outer layer of foods (usually the skin) with a knife or other paring tool.
Poach	To cook (fish, eggs, etc.) in barely simmering liquid, basting frequently with that liquid until done.
Simmer	To cook in liquid just below the boiling point; bubbles can just barely be seen under the surface of the liquid.
Sliver	To cut into long thin pieces; e.g., slivered almonds.
Snip	To cut into very tiny pieces with scissors; e.g., fresh parsley, chives.
Stir-fry	To cook meat or vegetables in small amounts of oil in a wok or heavy frypan over high heat until tender crisp.
Whip	To beat rapidly with wire whisk or electric beater to incorporate air.

Company Meals

All starred items can be made up all or in part, ahead of time.

Instant Squash Bisque page 89*
Slow Cooker Roast Chicken page 126*
with...
Chestnut Dressing page 111*
Buttered Peas and Carrots
Mashed Potatoes page 102*
Sliced avocado on lettuce leaves
with...
Blue Cheese Dressing page 150*
Croissants (from freezer) page 80*
Magic Crust Maple Walnut Pie
page 168*
Beverage of choice

❏ ❏ ❏

Slow Cooker Prime Rib Roast of Beef
page 136*
Beefy Rice and Mushrooms page 99*
Twenty-four Hour Salad page 147*
Mashed turnip
(peel and cook ahead; reheat)*
Cloverleaf rolls (from freezer)
page 78*
Magic Crust Cheesecake page 166*
Beverage of choice

❏ ❏ ❏

More Menus

Slow Cooker Beef Stroganoff
page 135*
Buttered Noodles
French bread (from freezer) page 82*
Three-bean salad*
Buttered corn
Magic Crust Pumpkin Pie
page 166*
Beverage of choice

❏ ❏ ❏

Super Quick Spanish Rice w/Beef
page 97*
Tossed fresh vegetable salad with
favorite dressing*
Bran muffins page 69*
Fresh fruit of choice*
Beverage of choice

❏ ❏ ❏

Baked Cheese and Onion Fondue
page 114*
Stir Fried Zucchini Sticks
French bread (from freezer) page 82*
Buttered fresh carrots (peeled ahead)
Chocolate Chip Cookies page 171*
Beverage of choice

❏ ❏ ❏

Holiday Turkey Pie page 133*
Slow Cooker Baked Potatoes
page 103*
Frozen Fruit Salad on lettuce
page 148*
Croissants (from freezer) page 80*
Fudgie Brownies page 159*
Beverage of choice

□ □ □

Overnight Crabmeat Casserole
page 115*
Twenty-four Hour Salad page 147*
Homemade bread (from freezer) page 72*
Mashed winter squash
Peanut Butter Cookies page 170*
Beverage of choice

□ □ □

Mexicali Omelet page 108 with...
South of the Border Salsa page 154*
Cornbread with chilies page 79
Buttered green beans
Molded Orange Pineapple Cream
page 173*
Beverage of choice

□ □ □

Chicken Divan Quickie page 132
Bran Muffins page 69*
Cabbage, Carrot and Raisin Salad
page 149*
Chocolate Cake with whipped
topping page 160*
Beverage of choice

□ □ □

Magic Crust Seafood Pie page 122*
Buttered Broccoli
Sliced tomatoes and cucumbers
Bread and butter
Fruited Mousse page 174*
Beverage of choice

□ □ □

INDEX

A

Appliances, 3–15
  large, 3–7
  small, 7–15
  using, 17–19
Apricot Sauce, Brandied, Roast Duckling with, 127
Automatic bag sealers, 12–13
Automatic timers, 13
Avocado Soup, Iced, 87

B

Bag sealers, automatic, 12–13
Baked Beans, Slow-Cooker, 106
Baked Cheese and Onion Fondue, 114
Baked Cod with Shrimp Sauce, 116
Baked Ham with Pineapple, 145
Baked Oriental Fish, 120
Baked Potatoes
  Microwave-to-Oven, 104
  Slow-Cooker, 103
Baked Stuffed Fillet of Sole, 117
Baking Powder Biscuit Mix, 70
Baking Powder Biscuits, 73
Bean(s)
  Bake, Cheddary Ham and, 107
  Baked, Slow-Cooker, 106
  dried, cooking in a slow-cooker, 19
Beef
  Beefy Rice and Mushrooms, 99
  broth, freezing, 15–16
  Ground, and Pasta Soup, 94
  Meatballs, Big-Batch, 137
  Meat Loaf, 142
  Pot Roast with Vegetable Gravy, 138–139
  Prime Rib Roast of, Slow-Cooker, 136
  and Snowpeas, Stir-Fried, 141
  Spanish Rice with, Super-Quick, 97
  Stew, Slow-Cooker, 140
  Stir-fry, Last Minute, 139
  Stock, Homemade, 86
  Stroganoff, Slow-Cooker, 135
Beefy Rice and Mushrooms, 99
Big-Batch Meatballs, 137
Biscuit(s)
  Baking Powder, 73
  Mix, Baking Powder, 70
  shortcake, 73
Bisque, Instant Squash, 89
Blenders, 11
Blue Cheese Dressing, 150
Boiled Dinner, Slow-Cooker, New-Fashioned, 128–129
Bran Muffins, 71
Brandied Apricot Sauce, Roast Duckling with, 127
Bread(s), 69
  Brown-and-Serve, 74
  Cornbread, 79
    Double-Corn, 79
    Mexican, 79
    mix, 70
  freezing, 17
  French, Quick-and-Easy, 82–83
  Homemade, 72–73
  mix
    cornbread, 70
    homemade, 63
  Pumpkin, 77
  Stuffing, Homemade, 76
  tips, 30–32
Broccoli
  Quiche, Crustless, 109
  Soup, Cauliflower, and Cheddar, 95
Broth. *See also* Soup(s)
  cooking, 28
  cooking in a slow-cooker, 20
  freezing, 15–16
  Rich Chicken, 85
Brown-and-Serve Bread, 74
Brownie Hot Fudge Sundae, 163
Brownies, Fudge, 159
Buns, Sticky, 84
Buttermilk Dressing, 149

C

Cabbage, Carrot, and Raisin Salad, 149
Cake
  Cheesecake, Magic Crust, 166–167
  Chocolate, Mix, 63
  Chocolate, Quick-and-Easy, 160–161
  Peach Shortcake, Rich, 169
Carrot, and Raisin Salad, Cabbage, 149
Casserole(s)
  Broccoli Quiche, Crustless, 109
  Cheese and Onion Fondue, Baked, 114
  cooking in a microwave oven, 24

cooking in a slow-cooker, 21, 22
Crabmeat, Overnight, 115
freezing, 16
Ham and Bean Bake, Cheddary, 107
Lasagna, Slow-Cooker, 110–111
Mexicali Baked Omelet, 108
Rice and Vegetable, Slow-Cooker, 98
Spanish Rice with Beef, Super-Quick, 97
Cauliflower
  and Cheddar Soup, Broccoli, 95
  Cheddar Soup, Super-Quick, 91
Celery leaves, storing, 33
Chain cooking, 35–51
  finishing food preparation, 50
  intermediate food preparation, 48–50
  preliminary food preparation, 46–48
Cheddar Soup
  Broccoli, Cauliflower, and, 95
  Cauliflower, Super-Quick, 91
Cheddary Ham and Bean Bake, 107
Cheese. *See also* specific cheeses
  and Onion Fondue, Baked, 114
  processed, 59–60
    cooking in a slow-cooker, 21
  sauce
    cooking in a microwave oven, 25
    super-quick, 154
  Soup, Tomato, 90
  storing, 32
  Velveeta, 59–60
Cheesecake, Magic Crust, 166–167
Cheesey Scalloped Potatoes, 105
Chestnut(s)
  cooking in a microwave oven, 25
  Stuffing, 111
Chicken
  Boiled Dinner, Slow-Cooker New-Fashioned, 128–129
  broth
    freezing, 15–16

Rich, 85
cooking in a slow-cooker, 20
Divan Quickie, 132
Fricassee of, Slow-Cooker, 29
Fried, 124–125
  coating mix, 64
Oven Fried, 123
Pot Pie, 130
Roast, Slow-Cooker, 126
shopping tips, 27
Stir-Fried, and Vegetables, 125
Vegetable Soup, 96
Chocolate. *See also* Fudge
Cake
  mix, 63
  quick-and-easy, 160–161
Chip Cookies, 171
Cream Roll, 162–163
Frosting, Quick-and-Easy, 161
Fudge Pie, Magic Crust, 167
Chowder. *See also* Soup(s)
Corn, 90
Fish, 93
Cloverleaf Rolls, 78–79
Cocktail Sauce for Meatballs, 158
Cod with Shrimp Sauce, Baked, 116
Consommé, Instant Jellied, 88
Cookie(s)
  Chocolate Chip, 171
  Crisp Sugar, 171
  dough, freezing, 17
  Peanut Butter, 170
Cooking tips, 28–32
Corn Chowder, 90
Cornbread, 79
  Double-Corn, 79
  Mexican, 79
  mix, 70
Crabmeat Casserole, Overnight, 115
Cream puffs, tip for making, 32

Cream Roll, Chocolate, 162–163
Creamy Italian Dressing, 150
Crêpes, freezing, 17
Crisp Sugar Cookies, 171
Croissants, 80–81
  Brown-and-Serve, 80–81
Croutons, Seasoned, 75
Crumbs for Topping, 65
Crustless Broccoli Quiche, 109
Custard pie fillings, cooking tips, 30

D

Deep-fry units, electric, 14
Dessert(s), 159–174
  Brownies, Fudge, 159
  cake
    Cheesecake, Magic Crust, 166–167
    Chocolate, mix, 63
    Chocolate, Quick-and-Easy, 160–161
    Peach Shortcake, Rich, 169
  Cheesecake, Magic Crust, 166–167
  Cookies
    Chocolate Chip, 171
    Crisp Sugar, 171
    Peanut Butter, 170
  Cream Roll, Chocolate, 162–163
  Fruit Crisp, 172
  Fudge, 5-Minute, 164
  Mousse, Fruited, 174
  Orange Pineapple Cream, Molded, 173
  Pie
    Chocolate Fudge, Magic Crust, 167
    Maple Walnut, Magic Crust, 168
    Pumpkin, Magic Crust, 166
    Strawberry, 165
  Pudding, Instant Rice, 170
  Shortcake, Rich Peach, 169
  Sundae, Brownie Hot Fudge, 163
Dip, Herb, 158
Dishwashers, 6–7

using, 18-19
Double-Corn Cornbread, 79
Dough
   cookie, freezing, 17
   yeast, tips, 30-32
Dressing. *See* Salad, dressing
Duckling, Roast, with Brandied Apricot Sauce, 127

E

Egg(s)
   Drop Soup, instant, 89
   Mexicali Baked Omelet, 108
   storing tip, 33
Electric deep-fry units, 14
Electric fry-pan, 13-14
Electric ice crusher, 13
Electric knife, 14-15
Electric mixers, 11-12
End-of-the-Week (or Month) Vegetable Soup, 92
Entrées
   Beef and Snowpeas, Stir-Fried, 141
   Beef Stew, Slow-Cooker, 140
   Beef Stroganoff, Slow-Cooker, 135
   Boiled Dinner, Slow-Cooker New-Fashioned, 128-129
   Broccoli Quiche, Crustless, 109
   Cheddary Ham and Bean Bake, 107
   Cheese and Onion Fondue, Baked, 114
   Chicken Divan Quickie, 132
   Chicken, Fried, 124-125
   Chicken, Oven Fried, 123
   Chicken Pot Pie, 130
   Chicken and Vegetables, Stir-Fried, 125
   Cod with Shrimp Sauce, Baked, 116
   Crabmeat Casserole, Overnight, 115
   Duckling, Roast, with Brandied Apricot Sauce, 127
   Fricassee of Chicken, Slow-Cooker, 129
   Ham with Pineapple, Baked, 145
   Lamb Stew, 146
   Lasagna, Slow-Cooker, 110-111
   Meat Loaf, 142
   Mexicali Baked Omelet, 108
   Oriental Fish, Baked, 120
   Pizza, 112-113
   Pork Cutlet Parmesan, 144
   Pot Roast with Vegetable Gravy, 138-139
   Prime Rib Roast of Beef, Slow-Cooker, 136
   Rice and Vegetable Casserole, Slow-Cooker, 98
   Roast Chicken, Slow-Cooker, 126
   Roast Pork, Slow-Cooker, 143
   Scallops with Linguine, 121
   Seafood Newburg, Never-Fail, 119
   Seafood Pie, Magic Crust, 122
   Spanish Rice with Beef, Super-Quick, 97
   Stir-Fry, Last Minute, 139
   Stuffed Fillet of Sole, Baked, 117
   Tuna Tacos, Hot, 120
   Turkey Divan, Super-Quick, 131
   Turkey Pie, Holiday, 133
Equipment. *See also* Appliances
   basic kitchen, 4
   organizing, 45

F

Fillet of Sole, Baked Stuffed, 117
Fish, 115-122
   Chowder, 93
   Cod with Shrimp Sauce, Baked, 116
   cooking, 28-29
      in a microwave oven, 25
   Crabmeat Casserole, Overnight, 115
   Fillet of Sole, Baked Stuffed, 117
   Oriental Fish, Baked, 120
   Salmon Ring, 118
   Scallops with Linguine, 121
   Seafood Newburg, Never-Fail, 119
   Seafood Pie, Magic Crust, 122
   Tuna Tacos, Hot, 120
5-Minute Fudge, 164
Fondue, Baked Cheese and Onion, 114
Food, organizing, 44
Food processors, 7-9
   using, 30, 31
Freezer containers, 15
Freezers, 4-5
Freezing, 15-17
   breads, 17
   broth, 15-16
   casseroles, 16
   cookie dough, 17
   crêpes, 17
   fritters, 17
   gravies, 15
   onions, 17
   pancakes, 17
   rolls, 17
   sandwiches, 16
   sauces, 16
   sliced meats, 16
   soup, 16
   stocks, 15
   tomato paste, 15
   tray-, 15
   waffles, 17
French Bread, Quick-and-Easy, 82-83
French Dressing, Tomato Soup, 152
Fricassee of Chicken, Slow-Cooker, 129
Fried Chicken, 124-125
   Coating Mix, 64
   Oven, 123
Fried Rice, 100
   Instant, 101
Fritters, freezing, 17
Frosting, Chocolate, Quick-and-Easy, 161
Frozen Fruit Salad, 148
Frozen whipped topping, 60

Fruit
    Crisp, 172
        Topping, 65
    Salad, Frozen, 148
Fruited Mousse, 174
Fry-pan, electric, 13–14
Fudge
    Brownies, 159
    5-Minute, 164
    Hot, Sundae, Brownie, 163
    Pie, Magic Crust Chocolate, 167
    Sauce, Hot, 161

G

Garlic, tip, 30
Graham Cracker Pie Crust Mix, 66
Gravy
    freezing, 15
    Never-Fail, 156
    Vegetable, Pot Roast with, 138–139
Ground Beef and Pasta Soup, 94

H

Ham
    and Bean Bake, Cheddary, 107
    with Pineapple, Baked, 145
Herb Dip, 158
Herbed Rice Mix, Instant, 68
Herbs, storing, 32
Holiday Turkey Pie, 133
Homemade Beef Stock, 86
Homemade Bread, 72–73
    mix, 63
    stuffing, 76
Homemade mixes. *See* Mix(es)
Homemade Pie Crust Mix, 67
Hors d'oeuvre, Salmon Ring, 118
Hot Fudge Sauce, 161
Hot Fudge Sundae, Brownie, 163
Hot Tuna Tacos, 120

I

Ice cream, Brownie Hot Fudge Sundae, 163
Ice crusher, electric, 13
Ice packs, 15
Iced Avocado Soup, Instant, 87
Ingredient substitutions, 175–177
Instant Egg Drop Soup, 89
Instant Fried Rice, 101
Instant Herbed Rice Mix, 68
Instant Iced Avocado Soup, 87
Instant Jellied Consommé, 88
Instant Rice Pudding, 170
Instant Rice Soup, 87
Instant Squash Bisque, 89
Instant Sweet and Sour Sauce, 153
Italian Dressing, Creamy, 150

J

Jellied Consommé, Instant, 88

K

Kitchen equipment
    basic, 4
    organizing, 45
Kitchen, organizing
    equipment, 45
    food, 44
Knife, electric, 14–15

L

Lamb Stew, 146
Lasagna, Slow-Cooker, 110–111
Last Minute Stir-Fry, 139
Lettuce
    cooking, 30
    storing, 33
Linguine, Scallops with, 121

M

Magic Crust Cheesecake, 166–167
Magic Crust Chocolate Fudge Pie, 167
Magic Crust Maple Walnut Pie, 168
Magic Crust Pumpkin Pie, 166
Magic Crust Seafood Pie, 122
Main dishes. *See* Entrées
Maple Walnut Pie, Magic Crust, 168
Mashed Potatoes, 102
    cooking in a slow-cooker, 19
Meat. *See also* Meatballs; specific meats
    cooking, 28–29
    cooking in a microwave oven, 23–25
    cooking in a slow-cooker, 20
    freezing, 16
    loaf, cooking, 29, 142
    shopping tips, 28
    slicers, 14
Meatballs
    Big-batch, 137
    Cocktail Sauce for, 158
    Spaghetti Sauce for, 157
Menu plan, 53–57, 180–181
Mexicali Baked Omelet, 108
Mexican Cornbread, 79
Microwave ovens, 5–6
    using, 22–25
Microwave-to-Oven Baked Potatoes, 104
Mix(es), 61–68
    Baking Powder Biscuit, 70
    Chocolate Cake, 63
    Cornbread, 70
    Crumbs for Topping, 65
    Fried Chicken Coating, 64
    Fruit Crisp Topping, 65
    Graham Cracker Pie Crust, 66
    Homemade Bread, 63
    Homemade Pie Crust, 67
    Instant Herbed Rice, 68

Molded Orange Pineapple Cream, 173
Mousse, Fruited, 174
Muffins, Bran, 71
Mushrooms, Beefy Rice and, 99

N

Never-Fail Gravy, 156
Never-Fail Seafood Newburg, 119

O

Oil and Vinegar Dressing, 151
Omelet, Mexicali Baked, 108
Onion(s)
  cooking, 29
  Fondue, Baked Cheese and, 114
  freezing, 17
  storing, 33
Orange Pineapple Cream, Molded, 173
Oriental Fish, Baked, 120
Oster 8-quart Super-Pot, 14
Oven, tips for using, 18
Oven Fried Chicken, 123
Overnight Crabmeat Casserole, 115

P

Pancakes, freezing, 17
Pantry staples, 177
Parmesan, Pork Cutlet, 144
Parsley, storing, 33
Pasta
  homemade, 31
  Linguine, Scallops with, 121
  Sauce
    Quick-and-Easy, 157
    Spaghetti Sauce for Meatballs, 157
  Soup, Ground Beef and, 94
Pâté, Salmon Ring, 118
Peach Shortcake, Rich, 169
Peanut Butter Cookies, 170

Pie
  Chicken Pot, 130
  Chocolate Fudge, Magic Crust, 167
  crust
    cooking, 30
    mix, graham cracker, 66
    mix, homemade, 67
  custard fillings, cooking, 30
  Maple Walnut, Magic Crust, 168
  Pumpkin, Magic Crust, 166
  Seafood, Magic Crust, 122
  Strawberry, 165
  Turkey, Holiday, 133
Pineapple
  Baked Ham with, 145
  Cream, Molded Orange, 173
Pizza, 112-113
Pork
  Cutlet Parmesan, 144
  Roast, Slow-Cooker, 143
Pot Pie, Chicken, 130
Pot Roast with Vegetable Gravy, 138-139
Potato(es)
  Baked
    Microwave-to-Oven, 104
    Slow-Cooker, 103
  cooking, 29
  cooking in a microwave oven, 23, 25
  cooking in a slow-cooker, 22
  Mashed, 102
    cooking in a slow-cooker, 19
  Scalloped, 105
    Cheesey, 105
Poultry, 123-133. *See also* Chicken; Duckling; Turkey
Prime Rib Roast of Beef, Slow-Cooker, 136
Processed cheese, 59-60
  cooking in a slow-cooker, 21
Processed foods, 59-60
Pudding, Instant Rice, 170

Pumpkin
  Bread, 77
  Pie, Magic Crust, 166

Q

Quiche
  cooking, 30
  Crustless Broccoli, 109
Quick-and-Easy Chocolate Cake, 160-161
Quick-and-Easy Chocolate Frosting, 161
Quick-and-Easy French Bread, 82-83
Quick-and-Easy Pasta Sauce, 157

R

Raisin Salad, Cabbage, Carrot, and, 149
Recipes
  adapting to microwave cooking, 23
  adapting to slow-cooker cooking, 21
Refrigerator, tips for using, 17-18
Rice
  Fried, 100
  Instant, 101
  Mix, Instant Herbed, 68
  and Mushrooms, Beefy, 99
  Pudding, Instant, 170
  Soup, Instant, 87
  Spanish, with Beef, Super-Quick, 97
  and Vegetable Casserole, Slow-Cooker, 98
Rich Chicken Broth, 85
Rich Peach Shortcake, 169
Roast Duckling with Brandied Apricot Sauce, 127
Roast of Beef, Slow-Cooker Prime Rib, 136
Roast Pork, Slow-Cooker, 143
Roll(s)
  Brown-and-Serve Croissants, 80-81
  Chocolate Cream, 162-163
  Cloverleaf, 78-79
  Croissants, 80-81

freezing, 17
frozen, cooking, 30
Sticky Buns, 84

S

Salad
  Cabbage, Carrot, and Raisin, 149
  Dressing
    Blue Cheese, 150
    Buttermilk, 149
    Creamy Italian, 150
    Oil and Vinegar, 151
    Thousand Island, 151
    Tomato Soup French, 152
  Frozen Fruit, 148
  24-Hour, 147
Salmon Ring, 118
Salsa, South-of-the-Border, 154
Sandwiches, freezing, 16
Sauce(s). *See also* Gravy
  Brandied Apricot, Roast Duckling with, 127
  Cheese, Super-Quick, 154
  Cocktail, for Meatballs, 158
  freezing, 16
  Hot Fudge, 161
  Pasta, Quick-and-Easy, 157
  Salsa, South-of-the-Border, 154
  Shrimp, Baked Cod with, 116
  Spaghetti Sauce for Meatballs, 157
  for Stir-Fried Dishes, 155
  Sweet and Sour, Instant, 153
Scalloped Potatoes, 105
  Cheesey, 105
Scallops with Linguine, 121
Seafood. *See also* Fish
  Newburg, Never-Fail, 119
  Pie, Magic Crust, 122
Seasoned Croutons, 75

Shopping
  list, 41, 42–43
  tips, 27–28
Shortcake Biscuits, 73
Shortcake, Rich Peach, 169
Shrimp Sauce, Baked Cod with, 116
Side dish(es)
  Beefy Rice and Mushrooms, 99
  Chestnut Stuffing, 111
  Fried Rice, 100
    Instant, 101
  Potatoes
    Baked, Microwave-to-Oven, 104
    Baked, Slow-Cooker, 103
    Mashed, 102
    Scalloped, Cheesey, 105
  Slow-Cooker Baked Beans, 106
Slow-cooker(s), 9–11
  Baked Beans, 106
  Baked Potatoes, 103
  Beef Stew, 140
  Beef Stroganoff, 135
  Fricassee of Chicken, 129
  Lasagna, 110–111
  New-Fashioned Boiled Dinner, 128–129
  Prime Rib Roast of Beef, 136
  Rice and Vegetable Casserole, 98
  Roast Chicken, 126
  Roast Pork, 143
  using, 19–22
Snowpeas, Stir-Fried Beef and, 141
Sole, Fillet of, Baked Stuffed, 117
Soup(s), 85–96. *See also* Broth
  Avocado, Instant Iced, 87
  Broccoli, Cauliflower, and Cheddar, 95
  canned, cooking in a slow-cooker, 21
  Cauliflower Cheddar, Super-Quick, 91
  Chicken Broth, Rich, 85
  Chicken Vegetable Soup, 96
  Consommé, Instant Jellied, 88

  cooking, 28–30
  Corn Chowder, 90
  Egg Drop, Instant, 89
  End-of-the-Week (or Month) Vegetable, 92
  Fish Chowder, 93
  freezing, 16
  Ground Beef and Pasta, 94
  Rice, Instant, 87
  Squash Bisque, Instant, 89
  stock
    freezing, 15
    homemade beef, 86
    storing, 33
  Tomato Cheese, 90
South-of-the-Border Salsa, 154
Spaghetti Sauce
  for Meatballs, 157
  Quick-and-Easy Pasta Sauce, 157
Spanish Rice with Beef, Super-Quick, 97
Spices, storing, 32
Squash Bisque, Instant, 89
Steamer, 14
Stew
  Beef, Slow-Cooker, 140
  Lamb, 146
Sticky Buns, 84
Stir-Fried Beef and Snowpeas, 141
Stir-Fried Chicken and Vegetables, 125
Stir-Fried Dishes, Sauce for, 155
Stir-fry dishes, cooking tip, 29
Stir-Fry, Last Minute, 139
Stock
  freezing, 15
  homemade beef, 86
  storing, 33
Storing food, 32–33
Strawberry Pie, 165
Stuffing
  Chestnut, 111
  Homemade Bread, 76

cooking in a slow-cooker, 21
Substitutions for ingredients, 175–177
Sugar Cookies, Crisp, 171
Sundae, Brownie Hot Fudge, 163
Super-Quick Cauliflower Cheddar Soup, 91
Super-Quick Cheese Sauce, 154
Super-Quick Spanish Rice with Beef, 97
Super-Quick Turkey Divan, 131
Sweet and Sour Sauce, Instant, 153

T

Tacos, Hot Tuna, 120
Thousand Island Dressing, 151
Timers, automatic, 13
Tofu, cooking, 29
Tomato. *See also* Spaghetti Sauce
   Cheese Soup, 90
   paste, freezing, 15
   Soup French Dressing, 152
Tools, 3–25
Topping(s)
   Crumbs for, 65
   Fruit Crisp, 65
   making, 32
   whipped, frozen, 60
Tray-freezing, 15
Tuna Tacos, Hot, 120
Turkey
   Divan, Super-Quick, 131
   Pie, Holiday, 133
24-Hour Salad, 147

V

Vegetable(s). *See also* specific vegetables
   Casserole, Slow-Cooker Rice and, 98
   cooking tip, 30
   frozen, cooking in a slow-cooker, 19
   Gravy, Pot Roast with, 138–139

shopping tips, 27
Soup, Chicken, 96
Soup, End-of-the-Week (or Month), 92
Stir-Fried Chicken and, 125
storing, 33
cooking in a microwave oven, 24
cooking in a slow-cooker, 22
Velveeta, 59–60

W

Waffles, freezing, 17
Walnuts, storing, 33
Weekly menu plan, 53–57
Whipped topping, frozen, 60

Y

Yeast dough, 30–32